THE POEMS

OF

WINTHROP MACKWORTH PRAED

REVISED AND COMPLETE EDITION.

WITH A MEMOIR

BY THE REV. DERWENT COLERIDGE.

IN TWO VOLUMES.

VOL. II.

NEW YORK:
W. J. WIDDLETON, PUBLISHER.
M DCCC LXVI.

M'CREA AND MILLER, STEREOTYPERS.

CONTENTS OF VOL. II.

POEMS OF LIFE AND MANNERS.

PART I.

PART II.

POEMS WRITTEN IN EARLY YOUTH.

PRIZE POEMS, TRANSLATIONS, AND EPIGRAMS.

SONGS.

CHARADES AND ENIGMAS.

POEMS OF LIFE AND MANNERS.

PART I.

(Eton, 1820–1821.)

POEMS

BY

WINTHROP MACKWORTH PRAED.

THE EVE OF BATTLE.

"It is not yet near day. Come, go with me;
Under our tents I'll play the eavesdropper."
Shakspeare.

THE night comes on, and o'er the field
The moon shines bright on helm and shield;
But there are many on that plain
That shall not see her light again;
She looks serene on countless bands
Of mailèd breasts and steel-bound hands;
And shows a thousand faces there
Of courage high, and dark despair,
All mingled as the legions lie
Wrapped in their dreams of victory.
A lowering sound of doubt and fear
Breaks sudden on the startled ear,
And hands are clinched, and cheeks are pale,
And from bright blade and ringing mail

A thousand hands, with busy toil,
Clean off each ancient stain or soil;
Or spots of blood, where truth may read
For every drop a guilty deed.

Survey the crowds who there await,
In various mood, the shock of fate;
Who burn to meet, or strive to shun,
The dangers of to-morrow's sun.
Look on the husband's anxious tears,
The hero's hopes, the coward's fears,
The vices that e'en here are found,
The follies that are hovering round;
And learn that (treat it as you will)
Our life must be a mockery still.
Alas! the same caprices reign
In courtly hall, or tented plain;
And the same follies are revealed
In ball-room, and in battle-field.

Turn to yon open tent, and see
Where, drunk with youth and Burgundy,
Reclines, his midnight revel o'er,
The beau of battle, Theodore.
Before him, on his desk, he lays
The billet-doux of other days;
And while he reads his fancy lingers
On those white hands and witching fingers
That traced the darling signatures—

The "Yours till death," and "Truly yours:"
And as by turns they meet his eye,
He looks, and laughs, and throws them by.
Until, perchance, some magic name
Lights up a spark of former flame;
And then he ponders, in his trance,
On Mary's love-inspiring glance,
On Chloe's eye of glittering fire,
And Laura's look of fond desire.
Poor Theodore! if valiant breast,
And open heart, and song, and jest,
And laughing lip, and auburn hair,
And vow sent up by lady fair,
Can save a youthful warrior's life,—
Thou fall'st not in to-morrow's strife.

Look yonder!—on the dewy sward
Tom Wittol lies—a brother bard;
He lies and ponders on the stars,
On virtue, genius, and the wars;
On dark ravines, and woody dells,
On mirth and muses, shot and shells;
On black mustachios, and White Surrey,
On rhyme and sabres—death and Murray;
Until at last his fancy glows
As if it felt to-morrow's blows;
Anticipation fires his brain
With fights unfought, unslaughtered slain;
And on the fray that *is to be*

Comes forth a Dirge or Elegy;
And if he meets no heavier harm
To-morrow, from a foeman's arm,
Than cracked cuirass, or broken head,
He'll hasten from his fever's bed,
And, just broke loose from salve and lint,
Rush, like a hero, into print;
Heading his light and harmless prattle—
"Lines written on a field of battle."
Thou favoured bard, go boldly on;
The Muse shall guard her darling son;
And when the musket's steady aim
Is levelled at the pet of fame,
The Muse shall check the impious crime,
And shield thee with a ream of rhyme;
But if 'tis doomed, and fall thou must,
Since bards, like other men, are dust,
Upon the tomb where thou shalt sleep
Phœbus and Mars alike shall weep;
And he that loved, but could not save,
Shall write "Hic jacet" o'er thy grave.

What wight is that, whose distant nose
Gives token loud of deep repose?
What! honest Harry on the ground?
I' faith thy sleep is wondrous sound,
For one who looks, upon his waking,
To sleep "the sleep that knows not breaking."
But rest thee, rest! thou merriest soul

That ever loved the circling bowl;
I look upon his empty cup,
And sudden tears, uncalled, spring up;
Perchance in this abode of pother
Kind Harry may not drain another;
But still our comrades at the Bell
On Harry's prowess long shall tell,
And dignify, with well-earned praise,
The revelry of other days.
And then the merry tale will run
Of many a wager lost and won,
On many a jest, and many a song,
And many a peal of laughter long,
That from our jovial circle broke
At Harry's toast, or Harry's joke;
Again, at Fancy's touch restored,
Our old sirloin shall grace the board;
Again, at Fancy's touch, shall flow
The tap we drained an age ago.

And thou, the soul of fun, the life
Of noisy mirth, and playful strife,
Mayst sleep, in Honour's worm-worn bed,
The dreamless slumber of the dead.
But oft shall one sad heart, at least,
Think on the smile that never ceased
Its catching influence, till the earth
Closed o'er the lips that gave it birth.
I'll pour upon thy tranquil rest

The hallowed bowl of Meux's best;
And recollect, with smile and sigh,
Thy "beer with E, and bier with I."

Dazzle mine eyes? or do I see
Two glorious Suns of Chancery?
The pride of Law appears the first,
And next the pride of Moulsey Hurst.
Faithless and feeless, from the bar
Tim Quill is come to practise war:
Without a rival in the ring,
Brown Robert "peels" for Church and King.
Thus ever to your country's fights
Together go, ye kindred knights!
Congenial arts ye aye pursued;
"*Daylight*" ye studied to exclude;
And both of old were *known to Crib*,
And both were very apt to *fib*.
Together go; no foe shall stand
The vengeance of our country's brand,
When on his ranks together spring
Cross-buttocks and *cross*-questioning.

Sir Jacob arming! what despair
Has snatched him from his elbow-chair?
And hurried from his good old wine
The bachelor of fifty-nine!
What mighty cause has torn him thus
Unwilling from suburban *rus*,

Bade him desert his one-horse chaise,
His old companions, and "old ways;"
Give up his Baccalaurean tattle,
And quit the bottle for the battle?
Has he forgot, in martial ardour,
His wig, his tea-pot, and his larder?
Has he forgot—ungrateful Sub.—
Champagne, backgammon, and—the club?
Has he forgot his native earth,
His sofa, and his decent hearth?
Has he forgot his homely fare,
And her, the maid with yellow hair,
That dressed the meat, and spread the board,
Laid fuel on the fire, and poured,
In stream as sparkling as her eye,
From its green goal the Burgundy?
That Hebe, in thy native town,
Looks from her latticed window down,
And, when the newsman paces by,
Runs, with a sharp and fearful cry,
And cheek all pale, and eye all wet,
To seek thy name in the Gazette.
What fate has bid her master roam,
An exile, from his cheerful home?
What! has his landlord turned him out?
Is he gone mad with love—or gout?
Has Death imposed his finger bony
Upon his mistress—or his crony?
Have sober matrons ceased to praise

The lover of their youthful days?
Are belles less eager to command,
With wink and smile, his ready hand?
Fears he the sudden dissolution
Of club-house—or of constitution?
Has the last pipe of hock miscarried?
Has——I forget, last week he—*married.*

Thou, too, thy brilliant helm must don,
Etona's wild and wayward son,
Mad, merry Charles. While, beardless yet,
Thou look'st upon thy plume of jet,
Or smilest as the clouds of night
Are drifted back by morning's light,
Thy boyish look, thy careless eyes,
Might wake the envy of the wise.
Six months have passed since thou didst rove,
Unwilling, through Etona's grove,
Trembling at many an ancient face
That met thee in that holy place;
To speak the plain and honest truth,
Thou wast no scholar in thy youth.
But now go forth—broke loose from school,
Kill and destroy by classic rule,
Or die in fight, to live in story,
As valiant Hector did before ye.
On! on! take forts, and storm positions,
Break Frenchmen's heads—instead of Priscian's,
And seek in death and conflagration

A *gradus* to thy reputation.
Yet when the war is loud and high,
Thine old mistakes will round thee fly;
And still, in spite of all thy care,
False quantities will haunt thee there,
For thou wilt make, amidst the throng,
Or *ζωή* short, or *κλέος* long.

Methinks I know that figure bold,
And stalwart limbs of giant mould!
'Tis he—I now his ruddy face,
My tried, staunch friend, Sir Matthew Chase.
His snore is loud, his slumber deep,
Yet dreams are with him in his sleep,
And Fancy's visions oft recall
The merry Hunt, and jovial Hall—
And oft replace before his sight
The bustle of to-morrow's fight.
In swift succession o'er his brain
Come fields of corn, and fields of slain;
And, as the varying image burns,
Blood and blood-horses smoke by turns;
The five-barred gate, and muddy ditch,
Smolensko, and "the spotted bitch,"
Parisian puppies—English dogs,
"Begar" and "damme,"—beef and frogs,
In strange, unmeaning medley fly
Before poor Nimrod's wandering eye.
He speaks! what murmuring, stifled sounds

Burst from his throat: "Why, madam! zounds!
Who scared me with that Gorgon face?
I thought I saw my Lady Chase."

And thou, too, Clavering—Humour's son!
Made up of wisdom and of fun!
Medley of all that's dark and clear,
Of all that's foolish, all that's dear;
Tell me, what brings thee here to die,
Thou prince of eccentricity?
Poor Arthur! in his childhood's day
He cared so little for his play,
And wore so grave and prim a look,
And cried so when he missed his book,
That aunts were eager to presage
The glories of his riper age;
And fond mamma in him foresaw
The bulwark of the British law,
And Science, from her lofty throne,
Looked down and marked him for her own.
Ah! why did Flattery come at school
To tinge him with a shade of fool!
Alas! what clever plans were crossed!
Alas! how wise a judge was lost!
Without a friend to check or guide,
He hurried into fashion's tide,
He aped each folly of the throng,
Was all by turns, and nothing long;
Through varying tastes and modes he flew,

Dress—boxing—racing—dice—Virtù;
Now looking blue in sentimentals,
Now looking red in regimentals,
Now impudent, and now demure,
Now blockhead, and now connoisseur,
Now smoking at "The Jolly Tar,"
Now talking Greek with Doctor Parr;
A friend by turns to saints and sinners,
Attending lectures, plays, and dinners,
The Commons' House, and Common Halls,
Chapels of Ease, and Tattersall's;
Skilful in fencing and in fist,
Blood—critic—jockey—methodist;
Causeless alike in joy or sorrow,
Tory to-day, and Whig to-morrow,
All habits and all shapes he wore,
And loved, and laughed, and prayed, and swore:
And now some instantaneous freak,
Some peevish whim, or jealous pique,
Has made the battle's iron shower
The hobby of the present hour,
And bade him seek, in steel and lead,
An opiate for a rambling head.
A cannon-ball will prove a pill
To lull what nothing else can still;
And I, that prophesy his doom,
Will give him all I can—a tomb,
And o'er a pint of *half-and-half*,
Compose poor Arthur's epitaph:—

"Here, joined in death, th' observer sees
Plato—and Alcibiades;
A mixture of the grave and funny,
A famous dish of Salmagundi."

Allan M'Gregor! from afar
I see him, midst the ranks of war,
That all around are rising fast
From slumbers that may be their last;
I know him by his Highland plaid,
Long borne in foray and in raid,
His scarf, all splashed with dust and gore,
His nodding plume, and broad claymore;
I know him by that eagle eye,
Where foemen read their destiny;
I know him by that iron brow
That frowns not, burns not, quails not, now,
Though life and death are with the ray
That redly dawns upon to-day.
Woe to the wretch whose single might
Copes with dark Allan in the fight;
He knows not mercy—knows not fear;
The pibroch has to Allan's ear
A clearer and a sweeter note
Than mellow strains that blithely float
From lyre or lute, in courtly throng,
Whére Beauty smiles upon the song.
Of artful wiles against his foe
Nothing he knows, or cares to know;

Far less he recks of polished arts,
The batteries in the siege of hearts.
And hence the minions of the ton,
While fair and foolish dames look on,
Laugh at Old Allan's awkward bow,
His stern address, and haughty brow.
Laugh they?—when sounds the hollow drum,
And banded legions onward come,
And life is won by ready sword,
By strength to strike, and skill to ward,
Those tongues, so brave in woman's war,
Those cheeks, unstained by scratch or scar,
Shall owe their safety in the fight
To hoary Allan's arm of might.

Close to the Clansman's side is seen
Dame Fortune's soldier, James M'Lean.
I know him well—no novice he
In warfare's murderous theory;
Amidst the battle's various sound,
While bullets flew like hail around,
M'Lean was born; in scenes like this
He passed his earliest hours of bliss;
Cradled in war, the fearless child
Looked on the scene of blood, and smiled;
Toyed with the sabre of the Blues
Long ere he knew its hellish use;
His little fingers loved to feel
The bayonet's bright point of steel,

Or made his father's helmet ring
With beating up—"God save the King!"
Those hours of youthful glee are fled;
The thin gray hairs are on his head;
Of youth's hot current naught remains
Within the ancient warrior's veins.
Yet, when he hears the battle-cry,
His spirit beats as wild and high
As on the day that saw him wield
His virgin sword on battle-field;
The eve on which his comrades found him,
With England's colours wrapped around him,
His face turned upwards, and his hand
Still twined around his trusty brand,
As, spent with wounds, and weak with toil,
He lay upon the bloody soil.
E'en now, though swift advancing years
Might well decline this life of fears,
Though the deep scars upon his breast
Show claim to honourable rest,
He will not quit what time has made
His joy, his habit, and his trade.
He envies not the peasant's lot,
His cheerful hearth, and humble cot;
Encampments have to him become
As constant, and as dear a home.

Such are the hearts of steel, whom War
Binds in their cradle to his car,

And leaves them in their latter day,
With honour, medals, and half-pay,
Burdened with all the cares of life,
Repentance—asthma—and a wife.

And what am I, who thus can choose
Such subject for so light a muse?
Who wake the smile, and weave the rhyme
In such a scene, at such a time?
Mary, whose pure and holy kiss
Is still a cherished dream of bliss,
When last I saw thy bright blue eye,
And heard thy voice of melody,
And felt thy timid, mild caress,
I was all hope—all joyousness!
We parted—and the morrow's sun—
O God! my bliss was past and done;
The lover's hope, the husband's vow,
Where were they then? ah! where wert *thou?*

Mary! thou vision loved and wept,
Long years have passed since thou hast slept,
Removed from gaze of mortal eye,
The dreamless sleep of those that die:
Long years! yet has not passed away
The memory of that fatal day
When all thy young and faded grace
Before me lay in Death's embrace.

A throb of madness and of pain
Shot through my heart and through my brain;
I felt it then, I feel it now,
Though time is stamped upon my brow;
Though all my veins grow cold with age,
And o'er my memory's fading page
Oblivion draws her damning line,
And blots all images—save thine.

Thou left'st me—and I did become
An alien from my house and home;
A phantom in life's busy dream;
A bubble on misfortune's stream;
Condemned through varying scenes to rove,
With naught to hope, and naught to love;
No inward motive, that can give
Or fear to die, or wish to live.

Away! away! Death rides the breeze!
There is no time for thoughts like these;
Hark! from the foeman's distant camp
I hear their chargers' sullen tramp;
On! valiant Britons, to the fight!
On! for St. George, and England's right!
Green be the laurel—bright the meed,
Of those that shine in martial deed!
Short be the pang—swift pass the breath,
Of those that die a Soldier's death.

THE COUNTY BALL.

"Busy people, great and small,
Awkward dancers, short and tall,
Ladies, fighting which shall call,
Loungers, pertly quizzing all."
Anon.

THIS is a night of pleasure! Care,
I shake thee from me! do not dare
To stir from out thy murky cell,
Where, in their dark recesses, dwell
Thy kindred Gnomes, who live to nip
The rose on Beauty's cheek and lip.
Until, beneath their venomed breath,
Life wears the pallid hue of Death.
Avaunt! I shake thee from me, Care!
The gay, the youthful, and the fair,
From "Lodge," and "Court," and "House," and "Hall,"
Are hurrying to the County Ball.
Avaunt! I tread on haunted ground,
And giddy Pleasure draws around,
To shield us from thine envious spite,
Her magic circle! Naught to-night
Over that guarded barrier flies
But laughing lips and smiling eyes;

My look shall gaze around me free,
And like my look my line shall be;
While fancy leaps in every vein,
While love is life, and thought is pain,
I will not rule that look and line
By any word or will of thine.

The Moon hath risen! Still and pale
Thou movest in thy silver veil,
Queen of the night! the filmy shroud
Of many a mild, transparent cloud
Hides, yet adorns thee;—meet disguise
To shield thy blush from mortal eyes.
Full many a maid hath loved to gaze
Upon thy melancholy rays;
And many a fond, despairing youth
Hath breathed to thee his tale of truth;
And many a luckless rhyming wight
Hath looked upon thy tender light,
And spilt his precious ink upon it,
In Ode, or Elegy, or Sonnet.
Alas! at this inspiring hour
I feel not, I, thy boasted power!
Nor seek to gain thine approbation
By vow, or prayer, or invocation;
I ask not what the vapours are,
That veil thee like a white cymar;
Nor do I care a single straw
For all the stars I ever saw!

I fly from thee, I fly from these,
To bow to earthly Goddesses,
Whose forms in mortal beauty shine
As fair, but not so cold, as thine.

But this is foolish! Stars and Moon,
You look quite beautiful in June;
But, when a Bard sits down to sing,
Your beauty is a dangerous thing;
To muse upon your placid beam,
One wanders sadly from one's theme;
And when weak Poets go astray,
The stars are more in fault than they.
The Moon is charming! so, perhaps,
Are pretty maidens in mob-caps;
But, when a Ball is in the case,
They're both a little out of place.

I love a Ball! there's such an air
Of magic in the lustre's glare,
And such a spell of witchery
In all I hear, and all I see,
That I can read in every dance
Some relic sweet of old romance;
As Fancy wills, I laugh and smile,
And talk such nonsense all the while,
That when Dame Reason rules again,
And morning cools my heated brain,
Reality itself doth seem

Naught but the pageant of a dream;
In raptures deep I gaze, as now,
On smiling lip, and tranquil brow,
While merry voices echo round,
And music's most inviting sound
Swells on mine ear; the glances fly,
And love and folly flutter high,
And many a fair, romantic cheek,
Reddened with pleasure or with pique,
Glows with a sentimental flush,
That seems a bright, unfading blush;
And slender arms before my face
Are rounded with a Statue's grace:
And ringlets wave, and beauteous feet,
Swifter than lightning, part and meet;
Frowns come and go; white hands are pressed;
And sighs are heard, and secrets guessed,
And looks are kind, and eyes are bright,
And tongues are free, and hearts are light.
Sometimes upon the crowd I look,
Secure in some sequestered nook,
And while from thence I look and listen,
Though ladies' eyes so gayly glisten,
Though ladies' locks so lightly float,
Though Music pours her mellowed note,
Some little spite will oft intrude
Upon my merry solitude.

By turns the ever-varying scene
Awakes within me mirth and spleen;
By turns the gay and vain appear,—
By turns I love to smile and sneer,
Mixing my malice with my glee,
Good-humour with misanthropy;
And while my raptured eyes adore
Half the bright forms that flit before,
I notice with a little laugh
The follies of the other half.
That little laugh will oft call down,
From matron sage, rebuke and frown;
Little, in truth, for these I care,—
By Momus and his mirth I swear!
For all the dishes Rowley tastes,
For all the paper Courtenay wastes,
For all the punch his subjects quaff,
I would not change that little laugh.*

Shall I not laugh, when every fool
Comes hither for my ridicule;
When every face, that flits to-night
In long review before my sight,
Shows off, unask'd, its airs and graces,
Unconscious of the mirth it raises?

* —— Hoc ego opertum,
Hoc ridere meum, tam nil, nulla tibi vendo
Iliade. *Pers.*

Skilled to deceive our ears and eyes
By civil looks and civil lies,
Skilled from the search of men to hide
His narrow bosom's inward pride,
And charm the blockheads he beguiles
By uniformity of smiles,
The County Member, bright Sir Paul,
Is Primo Buffo at the Ball.

Since first he longed to represent
His fellow-men in Parliament,
Courted the cobblers and their spouses,
And sought his honours in mud-houses,
Full thirty Springs have come and fled;
And though from off his shining head
The twin destroyers, Time and Care,
Begin to pluck its fading hair,
Yet where it grew, and where it grows,
Lie powder's never-varying snows,
And hide the havoc years have made,
In kind monotony of shade.
Sir Paul is young in all but years,
And when his courteous face appears,
The maiden wall-flowers of the room
Admire the freshness of his bloom,
Hint that his face has made him vain,
And vow "he grows a boy again;"
And giddy girls of gay fifteen
Mimic his manner and his mien,

And when the supple politician
Bestows his bow of recognition,
Or forces on th' averted ear
The flattery it affects to fear,
They look, and laugh behind the fan,
And dub Sir Paul "the young old man."

Look! as he paces round, he greets,
With nod and simper, all he meets:—
"Ah! ha! your Lordship! is it you?
Still slave to Beauty and *beaux yeux?*
Well! well! and how's the gout, my Lord?—
My dear Sir Charles! upon my word,
L'air de Paris, since last I knew you,
Has been Medea's caldron to you:—
William! my boy! how fast you grow!
Yours is a light fantastic toe,
Winged with the wings of Mercury!
I was a scholar once, you see!
And how's the mare you used to ride?
And who's the Hebe by your side?—
Doctor! I thought I heard you sneeze!
How is my dear Hippocrates?
What have you done for old John Oates,
The gouty merchant with five votes?
What! dead? well! well! no fault of yours!
There is no drug that always cures!
Ah! Doctor, I begin to break,
And I'm glad of it, for *your* sake."

As thus the spruce M. P. runs on,
Some quiet dame, who dotes upon
His speeches, buckles, and grimace,
Grows very eloquent in praise.
"How can they say Sir Paul is proud?
I'm sure, in all the evening's crowd,
There's not a man that bows so low;
His words come out so soft and slow;
And when he begged me 'keep my seat,'
He looked so civil and so sweet."—
"Ma'am," says her spouse, in harsher tone,
"He only wants to keep his own."
Her Ladyship is in a huff,
And Miss, enraged at *Ma's* rebuff,
Rings the alarm in t'other ear:
"Lord! now, Papa, you're too severe;
Where in the country will you see
Manners so taking, and so free?"
"His manners free? I only know
Our votes have made his letters so!"
"And then he talks with so much ease—
And then he gives such promises."
"Gives promises? and well he may!
You know they're all he gives away!"
"How folks misrepresent Sir Paul!"
"'Tis he misrepresents us all!"
"How very stale! but you'll confess
He has a charming taste in dress;
And uses such delightful scent;

And when he pays a compliment—"
"Eh! and what then, my pretty pet?
What then?—he never pays a debt!"

Sir Paul is skilled in all the tricks
Of politesse, and politics;
Long hath he learned to wear a mien
So still, so open, so serene,
That strangers in those features grave
Would strive in vain to read a knave.
Alas! it is believed by all
There is more "Sir" than "Saint" in Paul;
He knows the value of a place;
Can give a promise with a grace;
Is quite an adept at excuse;
Sees when a vote will be of use;
And, if the Independents flinch,
Can help his Lordship at a pinch.
Acutely doth he read the fate
Of deep intrigues, and plans of State;
And if, perchance, some powdered Peer
Hath gained or lost the Monarch's ear,
Foretells, without a shade of doubt,
The comings in, and goings out.
When placemen of distinguished note
Mistake, mislead, misname, misquote,
Confound the Papist and the Turk,
Or murder Sheridan and Burke,
Or make a riddle of the laws,
Sir Paul grows hoarse in his applause:

And when, in words of equal size,
Some oppositionist replies,
And talks of taxes and starvation,
And Catholic emancipation,
The Knight, in indolent repose,
Looks only to the ayes and noes.
Let youth say "grand!" Sir Paul says "stuff!"
Let youth take fire!—Sir Paul takes snuff.

Methinks, amid the crowded room,
I see one countenance of gloom;
Whence is young Edmund's pain or pique?
Whence is the paleness of his cheek?
And whence the wrathful eye, that now
Lowers, like Kean's, beneath the brow;
And now again on earth is bent,
'Twixt anger and embarrassment?
Is he poetical—or sad?
Really—or fashionably mad?
Are his young spirits colder grown
At Ellen's—or the Muses' frown?
He did not love in other days
To wear the sullens on his face,
When merry sights and sounds were near;
Nor on his unregarding ear
Unheeded thus was wont to fall
The music of the County Ball.

I pity all whom Fate unites
To vulgar Belles on gala-nights;

But chiefly him who haply sees
The day-star of his destinies—
The Beauty of his fondest dreaming,
Sitting in solitude, and seeming
To lift her dark, capricious eye
Beneath its fringe reproachingly.
Alas! my luckless friend is tied
To the fair Hoyden by his side,
Who opens, without law or rule,
The treasures of the Boarding-school:
And she is prating learnedly
Of Logic and of Chemistry,
Describing chart and definition
With geographical precision,
Culling her words, as bid by chance,
From England, Italy, or France,
Until, like many a clever dunce,
She murders all the three at once.
Sometimes she mixes by the ounce
Discussions deep on frill and flounce;
Points out the stains that stick, like burrs,
To ladies' gowns—or characters;
Talks of the fiddles, and the weather,
Of Laura's wreath, and Fannie's feather;—
All which obedient Edmund hears,
With passive look, and open ears,
And understands about as much
As if the lady spoke in Dutch;
Until, in indignation high,

She finds the youth makes no reply,
And thinks he's grown as deaf a stock
As Dido,—or Marpesian rock.*

Ellen, the lady of his love,
Is doomed the like distress to prove,
Chained to a Captain of the Wars,
Like Venus by the side of Mars.
Hark! Valour talks of conquered towns,
See! silent Beauty frets and frowns;
The man of fights is wondering now
That girls *won't* speak when dandies bow!
And Ellen finds, with much surprise,
That Beaux *will* speak when Belles despise;
"Ma'am," says the Captain, "I protest
I come to ye a stranger guest,
Fresh from the dismal, dangerous land,
Where men are blinded by the sand,
Where undiscovered things are hid
In owl-frequented pyramid,
And Mummies, with their silent looks,
Appear like memorandum-books,
Giving a hint of death, for fear
We men should be too happy here.
But if upon my native land
Fair ones as still as Mummies stand,
By Jove—I had as lief be there!"

* Dido—non magis—sermone movetur
Quam si dura silex, aut stet Marpesia cautes.—*Virg.*

(The lady looks—"I wish you were;")
"I fear I'm very dull to-night"—
(The lady looks—"You're very right;")
"But if one smile—one cheering ray"—
(The lady looks another way;)
"Alas! from some more happy man"—
(The lady stoops, and bites her fan;)
"Flattery, perhaps, is not a crime"—
(The lady dances out of time.)
"Perhaps e'en now, within your heart,
Cruel! you wish us leagues apart,
And banish me from Beauty's presence!"
The lady bows in acquiescence,
With steady brow and studied face,
As if she thought, in such a case,
A contradiction to her Beau
Neither polite—nor apropos.

Unawed by scandal or by sneer,
Is Reuben Nott, the blunderer, here?
What! is he willing to expose
His erring brain to friends and foes?
And does he venturously dare,
Midst grinning fop, and spiteful fair,
In spite of all their ancient slips,
To open those unhappy lips?

Poor Reuben! o'er his infant head
Her choicest bounties Nature shed;

She gave him talent, humour, sense,
A decent face and competence,
And then, to mar the beauteous plan,
She bade him be—an absent man.
Ever offending, ever fretting,
Ever explaining, and forgetting,
He blunders on from day to day,
And drives his nearest friends away.
Do Farces meet with flat damnation?
He's ready with "congratulation."
Are friends in office not *quite* pure?
He owns "he hates a sinecure."
Was Major ——, in foreign strife,
Not *over* prodigal of life?
He talks about "the coward's grave;"
And "who so base as be a slave?"
Is some fair cousin made a wife
In the full autumn of her life?
He's sure to shock the youthful bride
With "forty years come Whitsuntide."

He wanders round! I'll act the spy
Upon his fatal courtesy,
Which always gives the greatest pain,
Where most it strives to entertain.
"Edward! my boy! an age has passed,
Methinks, since Reuben saw you last;
How fares the Abbey? and the rooks?
Your tenants? and your sister's looks?

Lovely and fascinating still,
With lips that wound, and eyes that kill?
When last I saw her dangerous face,
There was a lover in the case.
A pretty pair of epaulettes!
But then, there were some ugly debts!
A match? Nay! why so gloomy, boy?
Upon my life I wish 'em joy!"

With arms enfolded o'er his breast,
And fingers clinched, and lips compressed,
And eye whose every glance appears
To speak a threat in Reuben's ears,
That youth had heard; 'tis brief and stern
The answer that he deigns return;
Then silent on his homeward way,
Like Ossian's ghosts, he strides away.

Astonished at his indignation,
Reuben breaks out in exclamation:
"Edward! I mean—I really meant—
Upon my word—a compliment;
You look so stern! nay, why is this?
Angry because I flattered Miss?
What! gone? The deuce is in the man!
Explain, Sir Robert, if you can."—
"Eh! what? perhaps you haven't heard!—
Excuse my laughing!—how absurd!

A slight *faux pas!*—a trifle—merely!
Ha! ha!—egad, you touched him, nearly."

All blunderers, when they chance to make
In colloquy some small mistake,
Make haste to make a hundred more
To mend the one they made before.
'Tis thus with Reuben! through the throng
With hurried steps he hastes along;
Thins, like a pest, the crowded seats,
And runs a muck at all he meets;
Rich in his unintended satire,
And killing where he meant to flatter.
He makes a College Fellow wild
By asking for his wife and child;
Puts a haught Blue in awful passion
By disquisitions on the Fashion;
Refers a knotty case in Whist
To Morley, the Philanthropist;
Quotes to a Sportsman from St. Luke,
Bawls out plain "Bobby" to a Duke;
And while a Barrister invites
Our notice to the Bill of Rights,
And fat Sir John begins to launch
Into the praises of a haunch,
He bids the man of quibbles pause
By eulogizing "Spartan Laws;"
And makes the Epicure quite wroth
By eulogizing "Spartan Broth."

Error on Error grows and swells,
For, as a certain proverb tells,
"When once a man has lost his way,—"
But you have read it,—or you may.

Girt with a crowd of listening graces,
With expectation on their faces,
Chattering, and looking all the while
As if he strove to hide a smile
That fain would burst Decorum's bands,
Alfred Duval, the hoaxer, stands.
Alfred! the eldest born of Mirth!
There is not on this nether earth
So light a spirit, nor a soul
So little used to all control.
Frolic, and Fun, and Jest, and Glee,
Burst round him unremittingly;
And in the glances of his eyes
Ever his heart's good-humour flies,
Mild as the breezes of the South;
And while, from many a wiser mouth,
We drink the fruits of education,
The solid Port of conversation,—
From Alfred's lips we seem to drain
A ceaseless flow of bright Champagne.
In various shapes his wit is found;
But most it loves to send around,
O'er half the town, on Rumour's gale,
Some marvellously-fashioned tale,

And cheat the unsuspecting ear
With groundless hope or groundless fear.
To speak in civil words—his bent
Lies sadly to—Embellishment.
"Sir!" says Morality, "you know
You shouldn't flatter Falsehood so:
The Nurse that rocked you in your crib,
Taught you to loathe and scorn a fib,
And Shakspeare warns you of the evil,
Saying, 'Tell truth, and shame the Devil!'
I like, as well as you, the glances
Where gay Good-Humour brightly dances;
But when a man tells horrid lies,
You shouldn't talk about his eyes."
Madam! you'll think it rather odd
That, while I bow me to the rod,
And make no shadow of defence,
I still persist in my offence;
And great and small may join to blame
The echo of the Hoaxer's fame;
But be it known to great and small,—
I can't write sermons at a ball.

'Tis Alfred fills the public prints
With all the sly, ingenious hints
That fly about, begirt with cares,
And terrify the Bulls and Bears.
Unrivalled statesman! War and peace
He makes and breaks with perfect ease;

Skilful to crown and to depose,
He sets up kings and overthrows;
As if apprenticed to the work,
He ties the bowstring round the Turk,
Or makes the Algerine devout,
Or plagues His Holiness with gout,
Or drives the Spaniards from Madrid
As quick as Bonaparte did.
Sometimes at home his plots he lays,
And wildly still his fancy plays.
He pulls the Speaker from the Chair,
Murders the Sheriffs, or the Mayor,
Or drags a Bishop through the mire,
Or sets the Theatres on fire,
Or brings the weavers to subjection,
Or prates of mobs and insurrection.
One dash of his creative pen
Can raise a hundred thousand men;
They march! he wills, and myriads fall;—
One dash annihilates them all!

And now, amid that female rout,
What scandal doth he buzz about?
What grand affair or mighty name
Intrusts he to the gossip Fame?
Unchecked, unstayed, he hurries on
With wondrous stories of the Ton;
Describes how London ladies lose
Their heads in helmets, like the Blues;

And how the highest circles meet
To dance with pattens on their feet!
And all the while he tells his lie
With such a solemn gravity,
That many a Miss parades the room,
Dreaming about a casque and plume;
And vows it grievously must tire one
To waltz upon a pump of iron.

Jacques, the Cantab! I see him brood,
Wrapped in his mental solitude,
On thoughts that lie too deep, I wis,
For such a scene and hour as this.
Now shall the rivers freeze in May,
Coquettes be silent at the play;
Old men shall dine without a story,
And mobs be civil to a Tory!
All miracles shall well befall,
When Youth is thoughtful at a ball.

From thoughts that grieve, and words that vex,
And names invented to perplex;
From latent findings, never found;
And mystic figures, square and round;
Shapes from whose labyrinthine toil
A Dædalus might well recoil;
He steals one night—one single night,
And gives its moments to delight.

Yet still upon his struggling soul
The muddy wave of Cam will roll,
And all the monsters grim, that float
Upon that dark and mirky moat,
Come jabbering round him—dark equation,
Subtile distinction, disputation;
Notion, idea, mystic schism,
Assumption, proof, and syllogism;
And many an old and awful name
Of optic or mechanic fame.
Look! in the van stern Euclid shows
The Asses' Bridge upon his nose;
Bacon comes forward, sage austere,
And Locke and Paley both are there;
And Newton, with a spiteful hiss,
Points to his "*de Principiis.*"
Yet often, with his magic wand,
Doth Mirth dispel that hideous band;
And then, in strange confusion lost,
The mind of Jacques is tempest-tossed.
By turns, around it come and flee
The *dulce*, and the *utile;*
By turns, as Thought or Pleasure wills,
Quadratics struggle with Quadrilles;
And figures sour, and figures sweet,
Of problems—and of dances—meet;
Bisections fight with "*down the middles,*"
And chords of arcs with chords of fiddles;
Vain are the poor musician's graces;

His bass gives way to given bases;
His studied trill to shapely trine;
His mellowed shake to puzzling sine;
Each forming set recalls a vision
Of some enchanting proposition,
And merry "*Chassez-croisés huit*"
Is little more than Q. E. D.
Ah! Stoic youth! before his eye
Bright beauties walk unheeded by;
And while his distant fancy strays
Remote through Algebraic maze,
He sees, in whatsoe'er he views,
The very object he pursues,
And fairest forms, from heel to head,
Seem crooked as his x and z.
Peace to the man of marble!—
Hush!
Whence is the universal rush?
Why doth confusion thus affright
The peaceful order of the night,
Thwart the musicians in their task,
And check the schoolboy's *pas de basque?*
The Lady Clare hath lost a comb!—
If old Queen Bess, from out her tomb,
Had burst with royal indignation
Upon our scandalous flirtation,—
Darted a glance immensely chilling
Upon our waltzing and quadrilling,—
Flown at the fiddlers in a pet,
And bade them play her minuet,—

Her stately step, and angry eye,
Her waist so low, her neck so high,
Her habit of inspiring fear,
Her knack of boxing on the ear,—
Could ne'er have made the people stare,
Like the lost comb of Lady Clare!
The tresses it was wont to bind,
Joy in their freedom! unconfined
They float around her, and bedeck
The marble whiteness of her neck
With veil of more resplendent hue
Than ever Aphrodite threw
Around her, when, unseen, she trod
Before the sight of man or God.
Look how a blush of burning red,
O'er bosom and o'er forehead spread,
Glances like lightning; and aside
The Lady Clare hath turned her head,
As if she strove in vain to hide
That countenance of modest pride,
Whose colour many an envying fair
Would give a Monarch's crown to wear.
Persuasion lurks on woman's tongue—
In woman's smile, oh! raptures throng—
And woman's tears compassion move—
But oh! 'tis woman's blush we *love!*

Now gallantry is busy round!
All eyes are bent upon the ground!

And dancers leave the cheerful measure
To seek the lady's missing treasure.
Meanwhile some charitable Miss,
Quite ignorant what envy is,
Sends slowly forth her censures grave—
"How oddly beauties will behave!
Oh! quite an accident!—last year,
I think, she sprained her ankle here;
And then there were such sudden halts,
And such a bringing out of salts!"—
"You think her vain?"—"Oh, gracious! no!
She has a charming foot, you know!
And it's so pretty to be lame—
I don't impute the slightest blame—
Only that *very* careless braid!—
The fault is with the waiting-maid!
I merely mean—since Lady Clare
Was flattered so about her hair,
Her comb is always dropping out—
Oh! quite an accident!—no doubt!"

The Sun hath risen o'er the deep,
And fathers, more than half asleep,
Begin to shake the drowsy head,
And hint "it's time to be in bed."
Then comes chagrin on faces fair;
Soft hands are clasped in mimic prayer;
And then the warning watch is shown,
And answers in a harsher tone

Reply to look of lamentation,
And argument, and supplication;
In vain sweet voices tell their grief,
In speeches long, for respite brief;
Bootless are all their "Lord!" s and "La!" s,
Their "Pray, Papa!" s and "Do, Papa!" s;
"Ladies," quoth Gout, "I love my rest!
The carriage waits!—*eundum est.*"
This is the hour for parting bow,
This is the hour for secret vow,
For weighty shawl, and hooded cloak,
Half-uttered tale, and whispered joke.
This is the hour when ladies bright
Relate the adventures of the night,
And fly by turns from truth to fiction,
From retrospection to prediction:
They regulate, with unbought bounty,
The destinies of half the county;
With gypsy talent they foretell
How Miss Duquesne will marry well,
And how 'tis certain that the Squire
Will be more stupid than his sire,
And how the girl they cried up so,
Only two little months ago,
Falls off already, and will be
Really quite plain at twenty-three.
Now Scandal hovers laughing o'er them,
While pass in long review before them
The Lady that my Lord admires—

The gentleman that moves on wires—
The youth with such a frightful frown—
And "that extraordinary gown."
Now characters are much debated,
And witty speeches are narrated;
And Criticism delights to dwell
On conquest won by many a belle,
On compliments that ne'er were paid,
On offers that were never made,
Refusals—Lord knows when refused,
Deductions—Lord knows how deduced;
Alas! how sweetly Scandal falls
From lips of beauties—after Balls.

The music stops,—the lights expire,—
The dance is o'er,—the crowds retire;
And all those smiling cheeks have flown!
Away!—the rhymer is alone.
Thou, too, the fairest and the best,
Hast fleeted from him with the rest;
Thy name he will not, love! unite
To the rude strain he pours to-night;
Yet often hath he turned away
Amidst his harsh and wandering lay,
And often hath his earnest eye
Looked into thine delightedly,
And often hath his listening ear——
But thou art gone!—what doth he here?

TO JULIO,

ON HIS COMING OF AGE.

Julio, while Fancy's tints adorn
The first bright beam of manhood's morn,
The cares of boyhood fleet away
Like clouds before the face of day;
And see, before your ravished eyes
New hopes appear, new duties rise;
Restraint has left his iron throne,
And Freedom smiles on twenty-one.

Count o'er the friends whom erst you knew,
When careless boyhood deemed them true,—
With whom you wiled the lazy hours
Round fond Etona's classic towers,
Or strayed beside the learned mud
Of ancient Cam's meandering flood;
The follies that in them you view,
Shall be a source of good to you.

With mincing gait, and foreign air,
Sir Philip strays through park and square,
Or yawns in Grange's sweet recess,
In all the studied ease of dress;

Aptly the manling's tongue, I deem,
Can argue on a lofty theme,—
Which damsel hath the merrier eye,
Which fop the better-fancied tie,
Which perfume hath the sweetest savour,
Which soup the more inviting flavour;
And Fashion, at Sir Philip's call,
Ordains the collars rise and fall,
And shifts the Brummel's varying hue
From blue to brown, from brown to blue.

And hence the motley crowd who e'er
Bear Fashion's badge, or wish to bear,
From Hockley Hole to Rotten Row,
Unite to dub Sir Philip—beau.

And such is Fashion's empty fame—
Squire Robert loathes the very name;
The rockets hiss, the bonfires blaze,
The peasants gape in still amaze;
The field unploughed—the ox unyoked,
The farmer's mouth with pudding choked,
The sexton's vest of decent brown,
The village maiden's Sunday gown,
In joyful union seem to say,
"Squire Robert is of age to-day."

The bumpkins hurry to the Bell,
And clam'rous tongues in riot swell;

Anger is hot—and so is liquor;
They drink confusion to the Vicar—
And shout and song from lad and lass,
And broken heads—and broken glass,
In concert horrible, declare
Their loyal reverence for the heir.

Right justly may the youthful Squire
These transports in his slaves inspire;
At every fireside through the place
He's welcome as the curate's grace;
He tells his story, cracks his joke,
And drinks his ale "*like other folk;*"
Fearless he risks that cranium thick
At cudgelling and single-stick;
And then his stud!—why! far and wide
It is the county's chiefest pride!
Ah! had his steed no firmer brains
Than the mere thing that holds the reins,
Grief soon would bid the beer to run
Because the Squire's mad race was done,
Not less than now it froths away,
Because "the Squire's of age to-day."

Far different pomp inspired of old
The youthful Roman's bosom bold,
Soon as a father's honoured hand
Gave to his grasp the casque and brand,
And off the light prætexta threw,

And from his neck the bulla drew,
Bade him the toga's foldings scan,
And glory in the name of "Man."
Far different pomp lit ardour high
In the young German's eager eye,
When, bending o'er his offspring's head,
An aged sire, half-weeping, said,—
"Thy duty to thy father done,
Go forth—and be thy country's son."
Heavens! how his bosom burned to dare
The grim delight of manhood's war,
And brandish in no mimic field
His beaming lance and osier shield:
How his young bosom longed to claim
In war's wild tumult manhood's name,
And write it, midst the battle's foam,
In the best blood of trembling Rome!

Such was the hope, the barbarous joy,
That nerved to arms the German boy;
A flame as ardent, more refined,
Shall brightly glow in Julio's mind;
But yet I'd rather see thee smile
Grimly on war's embattled file,
I'd rather see thee wield in strife
The German butcher's reckless knife,
Thinking thy claims to manhood grow
From each pale corse that bleeds below;—
I'd rather view thee thus,—than see
A modern blockhead rise in thee.

Is it a study for a Peer
To breathe soft vows in lady's ear,
To choose a coat—or leap a gate,
To win an heiress—or a plate?

Far nobler studies shall be thine—
So Friendship and the Muse divine:
It shall be thine, in danger's hour,
To guide the helm of British power,
And, midst thy country's laurelled crown,
To mix a garland all thine own.
Julio, from this auspicious day,
New honours gild thine onward way;
In thee Posterity shall view
A heart to faith and feeling true,
And Fame her choicest wreaths shall blend
For Virtue's, and the poor man's friend.

TO JULIA,

PREPARING FOR HER FIRST SEASON IN TOWN.

Julia, while London's fancied bliss
Bids you despise a life like this,
While Chiswick and its joys you leave,
For hopes that flatter to deceive,
You will not scornfully refuse
(Though dull the theme, and weak the Muse)
To look upon my line, and hear
What Friendship sends to Beauty's ear.

Four miles from Town, a neat abode
O'erlooks a rose-bush, and a road;
A paling, cleaned with constant care,
Surrounds ten yards of neat parterre,
Where dusty ivy strives to crawl
Five inches up the whitened wall;
The open window thickly set
With myrtle, and with mignonette,
Behind whose cultivated row
A brace of globes peep out for show;
The avenue—the burnished plate,
That decks the would-be rustic gate,
Denote the fane where Fashion dwells,
—"Lyce's Academy for Belles."

'Twas here, in earlier, happier days,
Retired from Pleasure's weary maze,
You found, unknown to care or pain,
The peace you will not find again.
Here Friendships, far too fond to last,
A bright, but fleeting radiance cast
On every sport that Mirth devised,
And every scene that Childhood prized,
And every bliss, that bids you yet
Recall those moments with regret.

Those friends have mingled in the strife
That fills the busy scene of life,
And Pride and Folly—Cares and Fears,
Look dark upon their future years:
But by their wrecks may Julia learn
Whither her fragile bark to turn;
And, o'er the troubled sea of Fate,
Avoid the rocks they found too late.

You know Camilla: o'er the plain
She guides the fiery hunter's rein;
First in the chase she sounds the horn,
Trampling to earth the farmer's corn,
That hardly deigned to bend its head,
Beneath her namesake's lighter tread.
With Bob the Squire, her polished lover,
She wields the gun, or beats the cover;
And then her steed!—why! every clown

Tells how she rubs Smolensko down,
And combs the mane, and cleans the hoof,
While wondering hostlers stand aloof.

At night, before the Christmas fire,
She plays backgammon with the Squire;
Shares in his laugh, and in his liquor,
Mimics her father and the Vicar;
Swears at the grooms—without a blush
Dips in her ale the captured brush.
Until—her father duly tired—
The parson's wig as duly fired—
The dogs all still—the Squire asleep,
And dreaming of his usual leap—
She leaves the dregs of white and red,
And lounges languidly to bed;
And still, in nightly visions borne,
She gallops o'er the rustic's corn;
Still wields the lash—still shakes the box,
Dreaming of "sixes"—and the fox.

And this is bliss! The story runs,
Camilla never wept—save once,
Yes! once indeed Camilla cried—
'Twas when her dear Blue-stockings died.

Pretty Cordelia thinks she's ill—
She seeks her med'cine at Quadrille;
With hope, and fear, and envy sick,

She gazes on the dubious trick,
As if eternity were laid
Upon a diamond, or a spade.
And I have seen a transient pique
Wake, o'er that soft and girlish cheek,
A chilly and a feverish hue,
Blighting the soil where Beauty grew,
And bidding Hate and Malice rove
In eyes that ought to beam with love.

Turn we to Fannia—she was fair
As the soft fleeting forms of air,
Shaped by the fancy—fitting theme
For youthful bard's enamoured dream.
The neck, on whose transparent glow
The auburn ringlets sweetly flow,
The eye that swims in liquid fire,
The brow that frowns in playful ire,
All these, when Fannia's early youth
Looked lovely in its native truth,
Diffused a bright, unconscious grace,
Almost divine, o'er form and face.

Her lip has lost its fragrant dew,
Her cheek has lost its rosy hue,
Her eye the glad enlivening rays
That glittered there in happier days,
Her heart the ignorance of woe
Which Fashion's votaries may not know.

The city's smoke—the noxious air—
The constant crowd—the torch's glare—
The morning sleep—the noonday call—
The late repast—the midnight ball,
Bid Faith and Beauty die, and taint
Her heart with fraud, her face with paint.

And what the boon, the prize enjoyed,
For fame defaced, and peace destroyed?
Why ask we this? With conscious grace
She criticises silk and lace;
Queen of the modes, she reigns alike
O'er sarcenet, bobbin, net, vandyke;
O'er rouge and ribbons, combs and curls,
Perfumes and patches, pins and pearls;
Feelings and faintings, songs and sighs,
Small-talk and scandal, love and lies.

Circled by beaux behold her sit,
While dandies tremble at her wit;
The Captain hates "a woman's gab;"
"A devil!" cries the shy Cantab;
The young Etonian strives to fly
The glance of her sarcastic eye,
For well he knows she looks him o'er,
To stamp him "buck," or dub him "bore."

Such is her life—a life of waste,
A life of wretchedness—and *taste;*

And all the glory Fannia boasts,
And all the price that glory costs,
At once are reckoned up, in one—
One word of bliss and folly—*Ton.*

Not these the thoughts that could perplex
The fancies of our fickle sex,
When England's favourite, good Queen Bess,
Was Queen alike o'er war and dress.
Then ladies gay played *chesse*—and ballads,
And learned to dress their hair—and salads;
Sweets—and sweet looks were studied then,
And both were pleasing to the men;
For cookery was allied to taste,
And girls were taught to blush—and baste.
Dishes were bright—and so were eyes,
And lords made love—and ladies pies.

Then Valour won the wavering field,
By dint of hauberk and of shield;
And Beauty won the wavering heart,
By dint of pickle, and of tart.
The minuet was the favourite dance,
Girls loved the needle—boys the lance;
And Cupid took his constant post
At dinner, by the boiled and roast,
Or secretly was wont to lurk
In tournament, or needle-work.
Oh! 'twas a reign of all delights,

Of hot Sir-loins,—and hot Sir knights;
Feasting and fighting, hand in hand,
Fattened, and glorified the land;
And noble chiefs had noble cheer,
And knights grew strong upon strong beer;
Honour and oxen both were nourished,
And chivalry—and pudding flourished.

I'd rather see that magic face,
That look of love, that form of grace,
Circled by whalebone, and by ruffs,
Intent on puddings, and on puffs,—
I'd rather view thee thus, than see
"A Fashionable" rise in thee.
If Life is dark, 'tis not for you
(If partial Friendship's voice is true)
To cure its griefs, and drown its cares,
By leaping gates, and murdering hares,
Nor to confine that feeling soul,
To winning lovers—or the vole.

If these and such pursuits are thine,
Julia! thou art no friend of mine!
I love plain dress—I eat plain joints,
I cannot play ten-guinea points,
I make no study of a pin,
And hate a female whipper-in.

LAURA.

"For she in shape and beauty did excel
All other idols that the heathen do adore."

"And all about her altar scattered lay
Great sorts of lovers piteously complaining."
Spenser.

A LOOK as blithe, a step as light
As fabled nymph, or fairy sprite;
A voice, whose every word and tone
Might make a thousand hearts its own;
A brow of fervour, and a mien
Bright with the hopes of gay fifteen;
These, loved and lost one! these were thine,
When first I bowed at Beauty's shrine;
But I have torn my wavering soul
From woman's proud and weak control;
The fane where I so often knelt,
The flame my heart so truly felt,
Are visions of another time,
Themes for my laughter,—and my rhyme.

She saw, and conquered; in her eye
There was a careless cruelty,
That shone destruction, while it seemed
Unconscious of the fire it beamed.

And oh! that negligence of dress,
That wild, infantine playfulness,
That archness of the trifling brow,
That could command—we know not how,
Were links of gold that held me then,
In bonds I may not bear again;
For dearer to an honest heart
Is childhood's mirth than woman's art.

Already many an aged dame,
Skilful in scandalizing fame,
Foresaw the reign of Laura's face,
Her sway, her folly, and disgrace.
Minding the beauty of the day
More than her partner, or her play:—
"Laura a beauty? flippant chit!
I vow I hate her forward wit!"
("I lead a club!")—"Why, Ma'am, between us,
Her mother thinks her quite a Venus;
But every parent loves, you know,
To make a pigeon of her crow."
"Some folks are apt to look too high—
She has a dukedom in her eye."
"The girl is straight" ("we call the ace"),
"But that's the merit of her stays."
"I'm sure, I loathe malicious hints—
But—only look, how Laura squints!"
"Yet Miss, forsooth"—("who play'd the ten?")
'Is quite perfection with the men;

The flattering fools—they make me sick"—
("Well—four by honours, and the trick.")
While thus the crones hold high debate
On Laura's charms and Laura's fate,
A few short years have rolled along,
And—first in Pleasure's idle throng—
Laura, in ripened beauty proud,
Smiles haughty on the flattering crowd;
Her sex's envy—fashion's boast—
An heiress—and a reigning toast.

The circling waltz, and gay quadrille,
Are in or out, at Laura's will;
The tragic bard, and comic wit,
Heed not the critic in the pit,
If Laura's undisputed sway
Ordains full houses to the play;
And fair ones of an humbler fate,
That envy, while they imitate,
From Laura's whisper strive to guess
The changes of inconstant dress.
Where'er her step in beauty moves,
Around her fly a thousand loves;
A thousand graces go before,
While striplings wonder and adore;
And some are wounded by a sigh,
Some by the lustre of her eye;
And these her studied smiles insnare,
And those the ringlets of her hair.

The first his fluttering heart to lose,
Was Captain Piercy of the Blues;
He squeezed her hand,—he gazed and swore
He never was in love before;
He entertained his charmer's ear
With tales of wonder, and of fear;
Talked much and long of siege and fight,
Marches by day, alarms by night;
And Laura listened to the story,
Whether it spoke of love or glory;
For many an anecdote had he
Of combat, and of gallantry;
Of long blockades, and sharp attacks,
Of bullets, and of bivouacs;
Of towns o'ercome,—and ladies, too,—
Of billet—and of billet-doux;
Of nunneries and escalades
And damsels, and Damascus blades.

Alas! too soon the Captain found
How swiftly Fortune's wheel goes round;
Laura at last began to doze,
E'en in the midst of Badajoz;
And hurried to a game at loo
From Wellington and Waterloo:
The hero, in heroics left,
Of fortune, and a wife bereft,
With naught to cheer his close of day
But celibacy, and half-pay,

Since Laura and his stars were cruel—
Sought his quietus in a duel.
He fought and perished; Laura sighed,
To hear how hapless Piercy died;
And wiped her eyes, and thus expressed
The feelings of her tender breast:
"What! dead?—poor fellow—what a pity!
He was *so* handsome and *so* witty;
Shot in a duel, too!—good gracious—
How I did hate that man's mustachios!"

Next came the interesting beau,
The trifling youth—Frivolio;
He came to see, and to be seen,
Grace and good-breeding in his mien;
Shone all Delcroix upon his head,
The West End spoke in all he said;
And in his neckcloth's studied fold
Sat Fashion, on a throne of gold.
He came, impatient to resign
What heart he had, at Laura's shrine;
Though deep in self-conceit incased,
He learned to bow to Laura's taste;
Consulted her on new quadrilles,
Spot waistcoats, lavender, and gills;
As willed the proud and fickle fair,
He tied his cloth, and curled his hair;
Varied his manners—or his clothes,
And changed his tailor, or his oaths.

Oh! how did Laura love to vex
The fair one of the other sex!
For him she practised every art
That captivates and plagues the heart.
Did he bring tickets for the play?
No—Laura had the spleen to-day.
Did he escort her to the ball?
No—Laura would not dance at all.
Did he look grave?—"the fool was sad;"
Was he jocose?—"the man was mad."
E'en when he knelt before her feet,
And there, in accents soft and sweet,
Laid rank and fortune, heart and hand,
At Laura's absolute command,
Instead of blushing her consent,
She "wondered what the blockhead meant?"

Yet still the fashionable fool
Was proud of Laura's ridicule;
Though still despised, he still pursued,
In ostentatious servitude,
Seeming, like lady's lap-dog, vain
Of being led by Beauty's chain.
He knelt, he gazed, he sighed, and swore,
While 'twas the fashion to adore;
When years had passed, and Laura's frown
Had ceased to terrify the town,
He hurried from the fallen grace,
To idolize a newer face;

Constant to nothing was the ass,
Save to his follies—and his glass.

The next to gain the Beauty's ear
Was William Lisle, the sonneteer,
Well deemed the prince of rhyme and blank;
For long and deeply had he drank
Of Helicon's poetic tide,
Where nonsense flows, and numbers glide;
And slumbered on the herbage green
That decks the banks of Hippocrene.
In short—his very footmen know it—
William is mad—or else a poet.*
He came and rhymed; he talked of fountains,
Of Pindus, and Pierian mountains;
Of wandering lambs, of gurgling rills,
And roses, and Castalian hills;
He thought a lover's vow grew sweeter,
When it meandered into metre;
And planted every speech with flowers,
Fresh blooming from Aonian bowers.

"Laura, I perish for your sake,"—
(Here he digressed about a lake;)
"The charms thy features all disclose,"—
(A simile about a rose;)
"Have set my very soul on fire,"—

* "Aut insanit homo—aut versus facit."—*Hor.*
"All Bedlam—or Parnassus is let out."—*Pope.*

(An episode about his lyre;)
"Though you despise, I still must love,"—
(Something about a turtle dove;)
"Alas! in death's unstartled sleep,"—
(Just here he did his best to weep;)
"Laura, the willow soon shall wave
Over thy lover's lonely grave."
Then he began, with pathos due,
To speak of cypress, and of rue.
But Fortune's unforeseen award
Parted the Beauty from the Bard;
For Laura, in that evil hour,
When unpropitious stars had power,
Unmindful of the thanks she owed,
Lighted her taper with an ode.
Poor William all his vows forgot,
And hurried from the fatal spot,
In all the bitterness of quarrel,
To write lampoons—and dream of laurel.

Years fleeted by, and every grace
Began to fade from Laura's face;
Through every circle whispers ran,
And aged dowagers began
To gratify their secret spite:—
"How shocking Laura looks to-night!
We know her waiting-maid is clever,
But rouge won't make one young forever;
Laura should think of being sage,
You know—she's of a *certain* age."

Her wonted wit began to fail,
Her eyes grew dim, her features pale;
Her fame was past, her race was done,
Her lovers left her one by one;
Her slaves diminished by degrees,
They ceased to fawn—as she to please.
Last of the gay, deceitful crew,
Chremes, the usurer, withdrew;
By many an art he strove to net
The guineas of the rich coquette;
But (so the adverse fates decreed)
Chremes and Laura disagreed;
For Chremes talked too much of stocks,
And Laura of her opera-box.

Unhappy Laura! sadness marred
What tints of beauty time had spared;
For all her wide-extended sway
Had faded, like a dream, away;
And they that loved her passed her by
With altered or averted eye.
That silent scorn, that chilling air,
The fallen tyrant could not bear;
She could not live when none admired,
And perished, as her reign expired.

I gazed upon that lifeless form,
So late with hope and fancy warm;
That pallid brow, that eye of jet,

Where lustre seems to linger yet;
Where sparkled through an auburn tress
The last dim light of loveliness,
Whose trembling ray was only seen,
To bid us sigh for what had been.
Alas! I said, my wavering soul,
Was torn from woman's weak control;
But when, amid the evening's gloom,
I looked on Laura's early tomb;
And thought on her, so bright and fair,
That slumbered in oblivion there;
That calm resolve I could not keep,
And then I wept,—as now I weep.

THE CONFESSION OF DON CARLOS.

IMITATED FROM THE SPANISH.

Oh! tell not me of broken vow—
I speak a firmer passion now;
Oh! tell not me of shattered chain—
The link shall never burst again;
My soul is fixed as firmly here
As the red Sun in his career;
As Victory on Mina's crest,
Or Tenderness in Rosa's breast.
Then do not tell me, while we part,
Of fickle flame, and roving heart;
While Youth shall bow at Beauty's shrine,
That flame shall glow—that heart be thine.

Then wherefore dost thou bid me tell
The fate thy malice knows so well?
I may not disobey thee!—Yes!
Thou bidd'st me,—and I *will* confess:—
See how adoringly I kneel—
Hear how my folly I reveal;
My folly!—chide me if thou wilt,
Thou shalt not—canst not call it—*guilt.*
And when my faithlessness is told,
Ere thou hast time to play the scold,

I'll haste the fond rebuke to check,
And lean upon thy snowy neck,
Play with its glossy auburn hair,
And hide the blush of falsehood there.

Inez, the innocent and young,
First shared my heart, and waked my song;
We were both harmless, and untaught
To *love* as fashionables ought;
With all the modesty of youth,
We talked of constancy and truth;
Grew fond of Music, and the Moon,
And wandered on the nights of June,
To sit beneath the chestnut-tree,
While the lonely stars shone mellowly,
Shedding a pale and dancing beam
On the wave of Guadalquivir's stream.
And aye we talked of faith and feelings,
With no distrustings, no concealings;
And aye we joyed in stolen glances,
And sighed, and blushed, and read romances.
Our love was ardent and sincere,—
And lasted, Rosa—half a year!
And then the maid grew fickle-hearted,
Married Don José—so we parted.
At twenty-one, I've often heard,
My bashfulness was quite absurd;
For, with a squeamishness uncommon,
I feared to love a married woman.

Fair Leonora's laughing eye
Again awaked my song and sigh:
A gay intriguing dame was she;
And fifty Dons of high degree,
That came and went as they were bid,
Dubbed her the Beauty of Madrid.
Alas! what constant pains I took
To merit one approving look:
I courted Valour and the Muse,
Wrote challenges—and billet-doux;
Paid for Sherbet and Serenade,
Fenced with Pegru and Alvarade;
Fought at the Bull-fights like a hero,
Studied small-talk,—and the Bolero;
Played the guitar—and played the fool;
This out of tune—that out of rule.
I oft at midnight wandered out,
Wrapped up in love—and my capote,
To muse on beauty—and the skies,
Cold winds—and Leonora's eyes.
Alas! when all my gains were told,
I'd caught a Tartar—and a cold.
And yet perchance that lovely brow
Had still detained my captive vow;
That clear blue eye's enchanting roll
Had still inthralled my yielding soul;
But suddenly a vision bright
Came o'er me in a veil of light,
And burst the bond whose fetters bound me,

And brake the spell that hung around me,
Recalled the heart that madly roved,
And bade me love, and be beloved.
Who was it brake the chain and spell?
Dark-eyed Castilian?—*thou* canst tell!
And am I faithless?—woe the while,
What vow but melts at Rosa's smile?
For broken vows, and faith betrayed,
The guilt is thine, Castilian maid!

The tale is told, and I am gone!
Think of me, loved and only one,
When none on earth shall care beside
How Carlos lived, or loved, or died!
Thy love on earth shall be to me
A bird upon a leafless tree—
A bark upon a hopeless wave—
A lily on a tombless grave—
A cheering hope—a living ray,
To light me on a weary way.

And thus is Love's Confession done;
Give me thy parting benison;
And ere I rise from bended knee,
To wander o'er a foreign sea,
Alone and friendless,—ere I don
My pilgrim's hat, and sandal shoon—
Dark-eyed Castilian! let me win
Forgiveness sweet for venial sin;
Let lonely sighs and dreams of thee,
Be penance for my perjury.

THE BACHELOR.

T. QUINCE, ESQ., TO THE REV. MATTHEW PRINGLE.

You wonder that your ancient friend
Has come so near his journey's end,
And borne his heavy load of ill
O'er Sorrow's slough, and Labor's hill,
Without a partner to beguile
The toilsome way with constant smile,
To share in happiness and pain,
To guide, to comfort, to sustain,
And cheer the last, long, weary stage,
That leads to Death, through gloomy Age!
To drop these metaphoric jokes,
And speak like reasonable folks,
It seems you wonder, Mr. Pringle,
That old Tom Quince is living single.

Since my old crony and myself
Laid crabbed Euclid on the shelf,
And made our Congé to the Cam,
Long years have passed; and here I am,
With nerves and gout, but yet alive,
A Bachelor, and fifty-five.
Sir, I'm a Bachelor, and mean,
Until the closing of the scene,

Or be it right, or be it wrong,
To play the part I've played so long,
Nor be the rat that others are,
Caught by a ribbon or a star.

"As years increase," your worship cries,
"All troubles and anxieties
Come swiftly on: you feel vexation
About your neighbours, or the nation;
The gout in fingers or in toes,
Awakes you from your first repose;
You'll want a clever nurse, when life
Begins to fail you!—take a wife;
Believe me, from the mind's disease
Her soothing voice might give you ease,
And when the twinge comes shooting through you,
Her care might be of service to you."

Sir, I'm not dying, though I know
You charitably think me so;
Not dying yet, though you, and others,
In augury your learnèd brothers,
Take pains to prophesy events
Which lie some twenty winters hence.
Some twenty?—look! you shake your head,
As if I were insane or dead,
And tell your children and your wife,—
"Old men grow *very* fond of life!"

Alas! your prescience never ends
As long as it concerns your friends;
But your own fifty-third December
Is what you never can remember!

And when I talk about my health,
And future hopes of weal or wealth,—
With something 'twixt a grunt and groan,
You mutter in an under tone,
"Hark! how the dotard chatters still!*
He'll not believe he's old or ill!
He goes on forming great designs,—
Has just laid in a stock of wines,—
And promises his niece a ball,
As if gray hairs would never fall!
I really think he's all but mad."
Then, with a wink and sigh, you add,
"Tom is a friend I dearly prize,
But never thought him *over* wise!"

You—who are clever to foretell
Where ignorance might be as well,

* I must confess that Dr. Swift
Has lent me here a little lift:
For when *I* steal some trifling hits
From older and from brighter wits,
I have some touch of conscience left,
And seldom like to *hide* the theft.
This is my plan; I name no name,
But wish *all* others did the same.

Would marvel how my health has stood:
My pulse is firm, digestion good,
I walk to see my turnips grow,
Manage to ride a mile or so,
Get to the village chûrch to pray,
And drink my pint of wine a day;
And often, in an idle mood,
Emerging from my solitude,
Look at my sheep, and geese, and fowls,
And scare the sparrows and the owls;
Or talk with Dick about my crops,
And learn the price of malt and hops.

You say, that, when you saw me last,
My appetite was going fast,
My eye was dim, my cheek was pale,
My bread—and stories—both were stale,
My wine and wit were growing worse,
And all things else,—except my purse;
In short, the very blind might see
I was not what I used to be.

My glass (which I believe before ye)
Will teach me quite another story;
My wrinkles are not many yet—
My hair is still as black as jet—
My legs are full—my cheeks are ruddy—
My eyes, though somewhat sunk by study,
Retain a most vivacious ray,

And tell no stories of decay;
And then my waist,—unvexed, unstayed
By fetters of the tailor's trade,—
Tells you, as plain as waist can tell,
I'm most unfashionably well.

And yet *you* think I'm growing thinner!
You'd stare to see me eat my dinner!
You know that I was held by all
The greatest epicure in Hall,
And that the voice of Granta's sons
Styled me the Gourmand of St. John's;
I have not yet been found unable
To do my duty to my table,
Though at its head no Lady gay
Hath driven British food away,
And made her hapless husband bear
Alike her fury and her fare.
If some kind-hearted chum calls in,—
An extra dish, an older bin,
And John, in all his finery dressed,
Do honour to the welcome guest;
And then we talk of other times,
Of parted friends, and distant climes,
And lengthened converse, tale, and jest,
Lull every anxious care to rest;
And when unwillingly I rise,
With newly-wakened sympathies,
From conversation—and the bowl,

The feast of stomach—and of soul,
I lay me down and seem to leap
O'er forty summers in my sleep;
And youth, with all its joy and pain,
Comes rushing on my soul again;
I rove where'er my boyhood roved—
I love whate'er my boyhood loved—
And rocks, and vales, and woods, and streams,
Fleet o'er my pillow in my dreams.
'Tis true some ugly foes arise
E'en in this earthly Paradise,
Which you, good Pringle, may beguile
By Mrs. P.'s unceasing smile.
I am an independent elf,
And keep my comforts in myself.
If my best sheep have got the rot—
Or if the Parson hits a blot—
Or if young Witless prates of laurel—
Or if my tithe produces quarrel—
Or if my roofing wants repairs—
Or if I'm angry with my heirs—
Or if I've nothing else to do—
I grumble for an hour or two;
Riots, or rumours, unrepressed,
My niece, or knuckle, over-dressed,
The lateness of a wished-for post,
Miss Mackrell's story of the ghost,
New wines, new fashions, or new faces,

New bills, new taxes, or new places,
Or Mr. Hume's enumeration
Of all the troubles of the nation,
Will sometimes wear my patience out!
Then, as I said before—the gout—
Well, well, my heart was never faint—
And yet it might provoke a saint.

A r[illegible]e of bread, or fall of rain,
Sometimes unite to give me pain,
And oft my lawyer's bag of papers
Gives me a taste of spleen and vapours.
Angry or sad, alone or ill,
I have my senses with me still;
Although my eyes are somewhat weak,
Yet can I dissipate my pique
By Poem, Paper, or Review;
And though I'm dozy in my pew,
At Dr. Poundtext's second leaf,
I am not yet so very deaf
As to require the rousing noise
Of screaming girls and roaring boys.
Thrice—thrice accursèd be the day
When I shall fling my bliss away,
And, to disturb my quiet life,
Take Discord in the shape of wife!
Time, in his endless muster-roll,
Shall mark the hour with blackest coal
When old Tom Quince shall cease to see

The *Chronicle* with toast and tea,
Confine his rambles to his park,
And never dine till after dark,
And change his comfort and his crony,
For crowd and conversazione.

If every aiding thought is vain,
And momentary grief and pain
Urge the old man to frown and fret,
He has another comfort yet;
This earth has thorns, as poets sing,
But not forever can they sting;
Our sand from out its narrow glass
Rapidly passes!—let it pass!
I seek not—I—to check or stay
The progress of a single day,
But rather cheer my hours of pain
Because so few of them remain.
Care circles every mortal head,—
The dust will be a calmer bed!
From Life's alloy no Life is free,
But—Life is not eternity!

When that unerring day shall come
To call me from my wandering, home,—
The dark, and still, and painful day,
When breath shall fleet in groans away,
When comfort shall be vainly sought,
And doubt shall be in every thought,

When words shall fail th' unuttered vow,
And fever heat the burning brow,
When the dim eye shall gaze, and fear
To close the glance that lingers here,
Snatching the faint departing light,
That seems to flicker in its flight,
When the lone heart, in that long strife,
Shall cling unconsciously to life,—
I'll have no shrieking female by
To shed her drops of sympathy;
To listen to each smothered throe,
To feel, or feign, officious woe;
To bring me every useless cup,
And beg "dear Tom" to drink it up;
To turn my oldest servants off,
E'en as she hears my gurgling cough;
And then expectantly to stand,
And chafe my temples with her hand;
And pull a cleaner night-cap o'er 'em,
That I may die with due decorum;
And watch the while my ebbing breath,
And count the tardy steps of Death;
Grudging the Leech his growing bill,
And rapt in dreams about the will.
I'll have no Furies round my bed!—
They shall not plague me—till I'm dead!

Believe me! ill my dust would rest,
If the plain marble o'er my breast,

That tells, in letters large and clear,
"The Bones of Thomas Quince lie here!"
Should add a talisman of strife,
"Also the Bones of Jane his Wife!"

No; while beneath this simple stone
Old Quince shall sleep, and sleep alone,
Some Village Oracle, who well
Knows how to speak, and read, and spell,
Shall slowly construe, bit by bit,
My "*natus*" and my "*obiit*,"
And then, with sage discourse and long,
Recite my virtues to the throng:—

"The Gentleman came straight from College!
A most prodigious man for knowledge!
He used to pay all men their due,
Hated a miser—and a Jew,
But always opened wide his door
To the first knocking of the poor.
None, as the grateful Parish knows,
Save the Church-wardens, were his foes;
They could not bear the virtuous pride
Which gave the sixpence *they* denied.
If neighbours had a mind to quarrel,
He used to treat them to a barrel;
And that, I think, was sounder law
Than any book I ever saw.

The Ladies never used to flout him;
But this was rather strange about him,
That, gay or thoughtful, young or old,
He took no wife, for love or gold;
Woman he called 'a pretty thing,'—
But never could abide a ring!"

Good Mr. Pringle!—you must see
Your arguments are light with me;
They buzz like feeble flies around me,
But leave me firm, as first they found me.
Silence your logic! burn your pen!
The Poet says "we all are men;"
And all "condemned alike to groan!"
You with a wife, and I with none.
Well!—yours may be a happier lot,
But it is one I envy not;
And you'll allow me, Sir, to pray,
That, at some near-approaching day,
You may not have to wince and whine,
And find some cause to envy mine!

MARRIAGE.

What, what is Marriage? Harris, Priscian,
Assist me with a definition.—
"Oh!" cries a charming, silly fool,
Emerging from her boarding-school—
"Marriage is—love without disguises,
It is a—something that arises
From raptures and from stolen glances,
To be the end of all romances;
Vows—quarrels—moonshine—babes—but
hush!
I mustn't have you see me blush."

"Pshaw!" says a modern modish wife,
"Marriage is splendour, fashion, life;
A house in town, and villa shady,
Balls, diamond bracelets, and 'my lady;'
Then for finale, angry words,
'Some people 's—'obstinate 's—'absurd!'s
And peevish hearts, and silly heads,
And oaths, and 'bête 's and separate beds!"

An aged bachelor, whose life
Has just been sweetened with a wife,
Tells out the latent grievance thus:
"Marriage is—odd! for one of us

'Tis worse a mile than rope or tree,
Hemlock, or sword, or slavery;
An end at once to all our ways,
Dismission to the one-horse chaise;
Adieu to Sunday can, and pig,
Adieu to wine, and whist, and wig;
Our friends turn out,—our wife's are clapped
in;
'Tis 'exit Crony,'—'enter Captain.'
Then hurry in a thousand thorns,—
Quarrels, and compliments,—and horns.
This is the yoke, and I must wear it;
Marriage is—hell, or something near it!"

"Why, marriage," says an exquisite,
Sick from the supper of last night,
"Marriage is—after one by me!
I promised Tom to ride at three.—
Marriage is—'gad! I'm rather late;
La Fleur!—my stays! and chocolate!—
Marriage is—really, though, 'twas hard
To lose a thousand on a card;
Sink the old Duchess!—three revokes!
'Gad! I must fell the Abbey oaks:
Mary has lost a thousand more!—
Marriage is—'gad! a cursed bore!"

Hymen, who hears the blockheads groan,
Rises indignant from his throne,

And mocks their self-reviling tears,
And whispers thus in Folly's ears:

"O frivolous of heart and head!
If strifes infest your nuptial bed,
Not Hymen's hand, but guilt and sin,
Fashion and folly, force them in;
If on your couch is seated Care,
I did not bring the scoffer there;
If Hymen's torch is feebler grown,
The hand that quenched it was your own;
And what I am, unthinking elves,
Ye all have made me for yourselves!"

HOW TO RHYME FOR LOVE.

At the last hour of Fannia's rout,
When Dukes walked in, and lamps went out,
Fair Chloe sat: a sighing crowd
Of high adorers round her bowed,
And ever Flattery's incense rose
To lull the Idol to repose.
Sudden some Gnome, that stood unseen,
Or lurked disguised in mortal mien,
Whispered in Beauty's trembling ear
The word of bondage and of fear,—
"Marriage:"—her lips their silence broke,
And smiled on Vapid as they spoke—
"I hate a drunkard, or a lout,
I hate the sullens and the gout;
If e'er I wed—let danglers know it,—
I wed with no one—but a poet."

And who but feels a Poet's fire
When Chloe's smiles, as now, inspire?
Who can the bidden verse refuse
When Chloe is his theme and Muse?

Thus Flattery whispered round;
And straight the humorous fancy grew,
That lyres are sweet when hearts are true;

And all who feel a lover's flame
Must rhyme to-night on Chloe's name;
And he's unworthy of the Dame,
Who silent here is found.
Since Head must plead the cause of Heart,
Some put their trust in answer smart,
Or pointed repartee;
Some joy that they have hoarded up
Those Genii of the jovial cup,
Chorus, and Catch, and Glee.
And, for one evening, all prepare
To be "Apollo's chiefest care."

Then Vapid rose—no Stentor this,
And his no Homer's lay—
Meek victim of antithesis,
He sighed and died away:—
"Despair my sorrowing bosom rives,
And anguish on me lies;
Chloe may die while Vapid lives,
Or live while Vapid dies!
You smile! the horrid vision flies,
And Hope this promise gives;
I cannot live while Chloe dies,
Nor die while Chloe lives!"

Next Snaffle, foe to tears and sadness,
Drew fire from Chloe's eyes;
And, warm with drunkenness and madness,

He started for the prize.
"Let the glad cymbals loudly clash!
Full bumpers let's be quaffing!
No poet I! Hip! hip! here goes!—
Blow—blow the trumpet!—blow the—"
Here he was puzzled for a rhyme,
And Lucy whispered "nose" in time,
And so they fell a-laughing.

"Gods!" cried a Minister of State,
"You know not, Empress of my Fate,
How long my passion would endure,
If passion were a sinecure;
But since, in Love's despotic clime,
Fondness is taxed, and pays in rhyme,
Glad to retire, I shun disgrace,
And make my bow, and quit my place."

And thus the jest went circling round,
And ladies smiled and sneered,
As smooth Fourteen, and weak Fourscore,
Professed they ne'er had rhymed before,
And Drunkards blushed, and Doctors swore,
And Soldiers owned they feared:
Unwonted Muses were invoked
By Pugilists and Whips;
And many a Belle looked half provoked,
When favoured Swains stood dumb and choked,
And Warblers whined, and Punsters joked,
And Dandies bit their lips.

At last an old Ecclesiastic,
Who looked half kind, and half sarcastic,
And seemed, in every transient look,
At once to flatter and rebuke,
Cut off the sport with "Psha! enough;"
And then took breath, and then—took snuff.
"Chloe," he said, "you're like the moon!
You shine as bright, you change as soon!
Your wit is like the moon's fair beam,
In borrowed light 'tis o'er us thrown;
Yet, like the moon's, that sparkling stream
To careless eyes appears your own;
Your cheek by turns is pale and red;
And then (to close the simile,
From which, methinks, you turn your head,
As half in anger, half in glee)—
Dark would the night appear without you—
And—twenty fools have rhymed about you."

CHANGING QUARTERS.

A SKETCH.

"Ah! then and there was hurrying to and fro,
And gathering tears, and tremblings of distress!
* * * * * * *
And there was mounting in hot haste."

Byron.

Fair laughs the morn, and out they come
At the solemn beat of the rolling drum,
 Apparelled for the march;
Many an old and honoured name,
Young warriors, with their eyes of flame,
And aged veterans in the wars,
With little pay, and many scars,
And titled Lord, and tottering Beau,
Right closely wrapped from top to toe
 In vanity and starch.
The rising Sun is gleaming bright,
And Britain's flag is waving light,
And widely, where the gales invite,
 The charger's mane is flowing:
Around is many a staring face
Of envious Boor, and wondering Grace,
And Echo shouts through all the place,—
 "The Soldiers be a-going!"
Beauty and Bills are buzzing now

In many a martial ear,
And, midst the tumult and the row,
Is seen the Tailor's anxious bow,
And Woman's anxious tear.
Alas! the thousand cares that float
To-day around a scarlet coat!
There's Sergeant Cross, in fume and fret,
With little Mopsa, the coquette,
Close clinging to his side:
Who, if fierce Mars and thundering Jove
Had had the least respect for love,
To-day had been his bride—
And, midst the trumpet's wild acclaim,
She calls upon her lover's name
In beautiful alarm;
Still looking up expectantly
To see the tear-drop in his eye,
Still hanging to his arm;
And he the while—his fallen chop
Most eloquently tells
That much he wishes little Mop
Were waiting for—another drop,
Or hanging—somewhere else.

Poor Captain Mill! what sounds of fear
Break sudden on his startled ear!
On right and left, above, around him,
Tom, the horse-dealer, roars, "Confound him!
A pretty conscience his;

To ruin thus my finest bay,
And hurry off, like smoke, to-day,—
If there's no law, some other way,
  By Jove, he'll smart for this!"
Ah! fly, unhappy, while you can!
The Captain is a dangerous man,
  A right old Jockey's son!
Ah! fly, unhappy, while you may!
The Captain first knocks up the Bay,
  And then—knocks down the Dun!

Old Larry is as brave a soul
As ever drained an English bowl;
His head and heart alike are tried;
And when two comrades have applied
Or hand to sword, or lip to pewter,
Old Larry never yet was neuter.
But now the Hero (like a fool
Ripe from a milksop boarding-school,
  In love or fortune crossed),
Silent, and pale, and stupid, stands,
Scratches his head with both his hands,
  And fears the hostile Host.
Oh! can it be? are hearts of stone
So small, and soft, and silky grown,
  That Larry fears a lick?
Oh! wrong not thus his closing years,
'Tis not the Host of France he fears,
  But of the Candlestick.

The Brute is there!—in long array,
All clean set down from day to day,
The dreaded figures stalk;
The Veteran, with his honest blows,
Can settle well a Score of Foes,
But not a Score of Chalk.
Alas! alas! that warrior hot
Balls from ten-pounders feareth not,
But Bills for pennies three;
And if he trembles, well I wot
He would not care for Gallic shot,
So here he were shot-free.

Fat Will the Butcher, in a pet,
His furious fang hath sharply set
On luckless Captain Martinette,
And thus the booby cries:
"Don't kick.—As sure as eggs is eggs
You will not have me off my legs,
Captain, although you tries;
And you must know, good Sir, as how
I mean to ha' my money now,
Or know the whens and whys."
The little Captain, whom 'twould kill
To be a public scoff,
Shuffles, and whispers—"Honest Will,
For forty shillings is your bill—
Take twenty—and be off."
The Butcher, much a friend to fun,

And somewhat apt to laugh or pun,
  Stands grinning like his calves;
Till for his joke his debt he barters—
"Sir, Gemmen, when they change their quarters,
  Shouldn't do things by halves."

He, too, the pride of war, is there,
Victorious Major Ligonier.
A soldier he from boot to plume,
In tented field, or crowded room,
Magnanimous in martial guise,
He eats, and sleeps, and swears, and lies;
Like no poor cit the man behaves,
And when he picks his teeth, or shaves,
He picks his teeth with warlike air,
And mows his beard *en militaire.*
But look! his son is by his side,
More like a young and blushing bride
  Than one in danger's hour,
All madly doomed to run and ride,
And stem the Battle's whelming tide,
  And face its iron shower.
In peace too warm, in war too cold,
Although with girls he's very bold,
  With men he's somewhat shy;
Nature could not two gifts afford,
And so she did not make his sword
  So killing as his eye.

Is there an eye which nothing sees,
  In what it views to-day,
To whisper deeper thoughts than these,
  And wake a graver lay?
Ah, think not thus! when Lovers part,
When weeping eye and trembling heart
  Speak more than words can say;
It ill becomes my jesting song
To run so trippingly along,
And on these trifling themes bestow
What ought to be a note of woe.

I see young Edward's courser stand,
The bridle rests upon his hand;
But beauteous Helen lingers yet,
With throbbing heart, and eyelid wet;
And as she speaks in that sweet tone
Which makes the listener's soul its own,
And as she heaves that smothered sigh
Which Lovers cannot hear and fly,
In Edward's face looks up the while,
And longs to weep, yet seems to smile.

"Fair forms may fleet around, my love!
  And lighter steps than mine,
And sweeter tones may sound, my love!
  And brighter eyes may shine;
But wheresoever thou dost rove,
Thou wilt not find a heart, my love,

So truly, wholly thine,
As that which at thy feet is aching,
As if its very strings were breaking!

"I would not see thee glad, my love!
  As erst, in happier years;
Yet do not seem so sad, my love!
  Because of Helen's fears!
Swiftly the flying minutes move,
And though we weep to-day, my love,
  Heavy and bitter tears,
There'll be, for every tear that strays,
A thousand smiles in other days!"

REMINISCENCES OF MY YOUTH.

"There's not a joy the world can give, like that it takes away,
When the glow of early thought declines in feeling's dull decay."—*Byron.*

SCENE of my best and brightest years!
Scene of my childhood's joys and fears!
Again I gaze on thee at last;
And dreams of the forgotten past,
Robed in the visionary hues
That Memory flings on all she views,
Come fleeting o'er me!—I could look
Unwearied on this babbling brook,
And lie beneath this aged oak,
And listen to its raven's croak,
And bound upon my native plain,—
Till Fancy made me Boy again!
I could forget the pain and strife
Of manhood's dark, deceitful life;
I could forget the ceaseless toil,
The hum of cities, and the coil
That Interest flings upon our hearts,
As Candour's faded glow departs;
I could forget whatever care
It has been mine to see or share,

And be as playful and as wild
As when—a dear and wayward child—
I dwelt upon this fairy spot,
All reckless of a bitterer lot.
Then Glee was high, and on my tongue
The happy laugh of Folly hung,
And Innocence looked bright on Youth,
And all was bliss, and all was truth.

There is no change upon the scene,
My native plain is gayly green;
Yon oak still braves the wintry air,
The raven is not silent there;
Beneath my foot the simple rill
Flows on in noisy wildness still.
Nature hath suffered no decay;
Her lordly children! where are they?
Friends of my pure and sinless age,
The good, the jocund, and the sage;
Gone is the light your kindness shed,
In silence have ye changed or fled;
Ye and your dwellings!—yet I hear
Your well-known voices in mine ear,
And see your faces beaming round,
Like magic shades on haunted ground.

Hark! as they murmur down the dell,
A lingering tale those voices tell;
And while they flit in vacant air,

A beauteous smile those faces wear.
Alas! I turn my dreaming eyes,
The lovely vision fades and flies;
    The tale is done—
    The smile is gone—
I am a stranger,—and alone.

Within yon humble cottage, where
The fragrant woodbine scents the air,
And the neat door looks fair to view,
Seen through its leafy avenue,
The matron of the Village School
Maintained her ancient state and rule.
The dame was rigid and severe,
With much to love, but more to fear;
She was my nurse in infancy;
And as I sat upon her knee,
And listened to her stories, told
In dialect of Doric mould,
While wonders still on wonders grew,
I marvelled if the tale were true;
And all she said of valorous knight,
And beauteous dame, and love, and fight,
Enchanter fierce, and goblin sly,
My childhood heard right greedily.
At last the wand of magic broke,
The tale was ended; and she spoke
Of learning's everlasting well,
And said, "I ought to learn to spell;"

And then she talked of sound and sense;
Of verbs and adverbs, mood and tense;
And then she would with care disclose
The treasured Primer's lettered rows—
Whereat my froward rage spoke out,
In cry and passion, frown and pout,
And with a sad and loathing look,
I shrank from that enchanted book.

Oh! sweet were those untutored years,
Their joys and pains, their hopes and fears;
There was a freshness in them all
Which we may taste, but not recall.
No! man must never more enjoy
The thoughts, the passions of the boy,
The aspirations high and bold,
Unseen, unguided, uncontrolled;
The first ambition, and the pride
That youthful bosoms feel and hide;
The longings after manhood's sun,
Which end in clouds—as mine have done.

In yonder neat abode, withdrawn
From strangers by its humble lawn,
Which the neat shrubbery enshrouds
From scrutiny of passing crowds,
The Pastor of the Village dwelt:
To him with clasping hands I knelt,
When first he taught my lips to pray,

My steps to walk in Virtue's way,
My heart to honour and to love
The God that ruleth from above.
He was a man of sorrows;—Care
Was seated on his hoary hair;
His cheek was colourless; his brow
Was furrowed o'er, as mine is now;
His earliest youth had fled in tears,
And grief was on his closing years.
But still he met, with soul resigned,
The day of mourning; and his mind,
Beneath its load of woe and pain,
Might deeply feel, but not complain;
And Virtue o'er his forehead's snows
Had thrown an air of meek repose,
More lovely than the hues that streak
The bloom of childhood's laughing cheek;
It seemed to tell the holy rest
That will not leave the righteous breast,
The trust in One that died to save,
The hope that looks beyond the grave,
The calm of unpretending worth,
The bliss that is not of the earth.
And he would smile; but in his smile
Sadness would seem to lurk the while:
Child as I was, I could not bear
To look upon that placid air;
I felt the tear-drop in mine eye,
And wished to weep, and knew not why.

He had one daughter.—Many years
Have fleeted o'er me, since my tears
Fell on that form of quiet grace,
That humble brow, and beauteous face.
She parted from this world of ill
When I was yet a child: but still,
Until my heart shall cease to beat,
That countenance so mildly sweet,
That kind blue eye, and golden hair,
Eternally are graven there.
I see her still, as when she stood
In the ripe bloom of womanhood;
Yet deigning, where I led, to stray,
And mingle in my childhood's play;
Or sought my father's dwelling-place,
And clasped me in her fond embrace;
A friend—when I had none beside;
A mother—when my mother died.

Poor Ellen! she is now forgot
Upon the hearths of this dear spot;
And they, to whom her bounty came,
They, who would dwell upon her name
With raptured voice, as if they found
Hope, comfort, riches, in the sound,
Have ceased to think how Ellen fled:—
Why should they sorrow for the dead?
Perhaps, around the festive board,
Some aged chroniclers record

Her hopes, her virtues, and her tomb;
And then a sudden, silent gloom
Creeps on the lips that smiled before,
And jest is still, and mirth is o'er.
She was so beauteous in her dress
Of unaffected loveliness,
So bright, and so beneficent,
That you might deem some fairy sent
To hush the helpless orphan's fears,
And dry the widow's gushing tears.
She moved in beauty, like the star
That shed its lustre from afar,
To tell the wisest on the earth
The tidings of a Saviour's birth;
So pure, so cheering was her ray—
So quickly did it die away.

There came a dark, infectious Pest
To break the hamlet's tranquil rest;
It came—it breathed on Ellen's face;
And so she went to Death's embrace,
A blooming and a sinless bride,—
And how, I knew not—but she died.

I was the inmate of her home,
And knew not why she did not come
To cheer my melancholy mood;
Her father wept in solitude;
The servants wore a look of woe,

Their steps were soft, their whispers low;
And when I asked them why they sighed,
They shook their heads, and turned aside.

I entered that forbidden room!
All things were still! a deathlike gloom
Stole on me, as I saw her lie
In her white vest of purity.
She seemed to smile! her lips were wet,
The bloom was on her features yet:
I looked! at first I thought she slept—
But when her accents did not bless—
And when her arms did not caress—
And when I marked her quiet air,
And saw that soul was wanting there—
I sat me on the ground, and wept!

SURLY HALL.

"Mercy o' me, what a multitude are here!
They grow still, too, from all parts they are coming,
As if we kept a fair here!"—*Shakspeare.*

The sun hath shed a mellower beam,
Fair Thames, upon thy silver stream,
And air and water, earth and heaven,
Lie in the calm repose of even.
How silently the breeze moves on,
Flutters, and whispers, and is gone!
How calmly does the quiet sky
Sleep in its cold serenity!
Alas! how sweet a scene were here
For shepherd or for sonneteer;
How fit the place, how fit the time,
For making love, or making rhyme!
But though the sun's descending ray
Smiles warmly on the close of day,
'Tis not to gaze upon his light
That Eton's sons are here to-night;
And though the river, calm and clear,
Makes music to the poet's ear,
'Tis not to listen to the sound
That Eton's sons are thronging round.

The sun unheeded may decline,
Blue eyes send out a brighter shine;
The wave may cease its gurgling moan,
Glad voices have a sweeter tone;
For, in our calendar of bliss,
We have no hour so gay as this,
When the kind hearts and brilliant eyes
Of those we know, and love, and prize,
Are come to cheer the captive's thrall,
And smile upon his festival.

Stay, Pegasus,—and let me ask,
Ere I go onward in my task,
Pray, reader,—were you ever here
Just at this season of the year?
No?—then the end of next July
Should bring you with admiring eye,
To hear us row, and see us row,
And cry—"How fast *them* boys *does* go!"
For Father Thames beholds to-night
A thousand visions of delight:
Tearing and swearing, jeering, cheering,
Lame steeds to right and left careering,
Displays, dismays, disputes, distresses,
Ruffling of temper, and of dresses;
Wounds on the heart, and on the knuckles;
Losing of patience, and of buckles.
An interdict is laid on Latin,
And scholars smirk in silk and satin;

And dandies start their thinnest pumps,
And Michael Oakley's in the dumps;
And there is naught beneath the sun,
But dash and splash, and falls and fun.

Lord! what would be the cynic's mirth,
If fate would lift him to the earth,
And set his tub, with magic jump,
Squat down beside the Brocas clump!
What scoffs the sage would utter there,
From his unpolished elbow-chair,
To see the seamstress' handiwork,
The Greek confounded with the Turk,
Parisian mix'd with Piedmontese,
And Persian joined to Portuguese;
And mantles short, and mantles long,
And mantles right, and mantles wrong,
Misshaped, miscoloured, and misplaced,
With what the tailor calls—a taste.
And then the badges, and the boats,
The flags, the drums, the paint, the coats;
But more than these, and more than all,
The pullers' intermitted call—
"Easy!"—"Hard all!"—"Now pick her up!"
"Upon my life, how I shall sup!"
Would be a fine and merry matter,
To wake the sage's love of satire.
Kind readers, at my laughing age,

I thank my stars I'm not a sage;
I, an unthinking, scribbling elf,
Love to please others,—and myself;
Therefore I fly *a malo joco*,
But like *desipere in loco*,
Excuse me that I wander so;
All modern pens digress, you know.

Now to my theme! Thou Being gay,
Houri or goddess, nymph or fay,
Whoe'er, whate'er, where'er thou art,
Who, with thy warm and kindly heart,
Hast made these blest abodes thy care;
Being of water, earth, or air,
Beneath the moonbeam hasten hither,
Enjoy thy blessings ere they wither,
And witness, with thy gladdest face,
The glories of thy dwelling-place!

The boat puts off!—throughout the crowd
The tumult thickens; wide and loud
The din re-echoes; man and horse
Plunge onward in their mingled course.
Look at the troop: I love to see
Our real Etonian Cavalry;
They start in such a pretty trim,
And such sweet scorn of life and limb.
I must confess, I never found
A horse much worse for being sound;

I wish my Nag not wholly blind,
And like to have a tail behind;
And though he certainly may hear
Correctly with a single ear,
I think, to look genteel and neat,
He ought to have his two complete.
But these are trifles! off they go
Beside the wondering River's flow;
And if, by dint of spur and whip,
They shamble on without a trip,
Well have they done! I make no question
They're shaken into good digestion.

I and my Muse,—My muse and I,
Will follow with the Company,
And get to Surly Hall in time
To make a Supper and a Rhyme.
Yes! while the animating crowd,
The gay, and fair, and kind, and proud,
With eager voice and eager glance
Wait till the pageantry advance,
We'll throw around a hasty view,
And try to get a sketch or two.

First in the race is William Tag,
Thalia's most industrious fag:
Whate'er the subject he essays
To dress in never-dying lays,—
A chief, a cheese, a dearth, a dinner,

A cot, a castle, cards, Corinna,
Hibernia, Baffin's Bay, Parnassus,
Beef, Bonaparte, Beer, Bonassus,—
Will hath his ordered words and rhymes
For various scenes and various times,
Which suit alike for this or that,
And come, like volunteers, quite *pat.*
He hath his Elegy, or Sonnet,
For Lucy's bier, or Lucy's bonnet;
And celebrates, with equal ardour,
A Monarch's sceptre, or his larder.
Poor William! when he wants a hint,
All other Poets are his mint;
He coins his epic, or his lyric,
His satire, or his panegyric,
From all the gravity and wit
Of what the ancients thought and writ.
Armed with his Ovid and his Flaccus,
He comes like thunder to attack us;
In pilfered mail he bursts to view,
The cleverest thief I ever knew.
Thou noble Bard, at any time
Borrow my measure and my rhyme;
Borrow (I'll cancel all the debt)
An epigram or epithet;
Borrow my mountains, or my trees,
My paintings, or my similes;
Nay, borrow all my pretty names,
My real or my fancied flames—

Eliza, Alice, Leonora,
Mary, Melissa, and Medora;
And borrow all my "mutual vows,"
My "ruby lips," and "cruel brows;"
And all my stupors, and my startings,
And all my meetings, and my partings;
Thus far, my friend, you'll find me willing;
Borrow all things, save one—a shilling!

Drunken, and loud, and mad, and rash,
Joe Tarrell wields his ceaseless lash;
The would-be sportsman; o'er the sides
Of the lank charger he bestrides,
The foam lies painfully; and blood
Is trickling in a ruddier flood,
Beneath the fury of the steel
Projecting from his armèd heel.
E'en from his childhood's earliest bloom,
All studies that become a groom,
Eton's *spes gregis*, honest Joe,
Or knows, or would be thought to know;
He picks a hunter's hoof quite finely,
And spells a horse's teeth divinely.
Prime terror of molesting duns,
Sole judge of greyhounds and of guns,
A skilful whip, a steady shot,
Joe swears he is!—who says he's not?
And then he has such knowing faces
For all the week of Ascot races,

And talks with such a mystic speech,
Untangible to vulgar reach,
Of Sultan, Highflyer, and Ranter,
Potatoes, Quiz, and Tam O'Shanter;
Bay colts and brown colts, sires and dams,
Bribings and bullyings, bets and bams;
And how the favourite *should* have won,
And how the little Earl was *done;*
And how the filly failed in strength,
And how some faces grew in length;
And how some people,—if they'd show,
Know something more than others know.
Such is his talk; and while we wonder
At that interminable thunder,
The undiscriminating snarler
Astounds the ladies in the parlour,
And broaches, at his mother's table,
The slang of kennel and of stable.
And when he's drunk, he roars before ye
One excellent, unfailing story
About a gun, Lord knows how long,
With a discharge, Lord knows how strong;
Which always needs an oath and frown
To make the monstrous dose go down.
Oh! oft and oft the Muses pray
That wondrous tube may burst one day,
And then the world will ascertain
Whether its master hath a brain.
Then, on the stone that hides his sleep,

These accents shall be graven deep;
Or, "Upton"* and "C. B." between,
Shine in the "Sporting Magazine:"
"Civil to none, except his brutes,
Polished in naught, except his boots—
Here lie the relics of Joe Tarrell;
Also, Joe Tarrell's double-barrel!"

Ho!—by the muttered sounds that slip,
Unwilling, from his curling lip;
By the gray glimmer of his eye,
That shines so unrelentingly;
By the stern sneer upon his snout—
I know the Critic, Andrew Crout!
The Boy-reviler! amply filled
With venomed virulence, and skilled
To look on what is good and fair,
And find, or make, a blemish there.
For Fortune to his cradle sent
Self-satisfying Discontent;
And he hath caught from cold Reviews,
The one great talent, to abuse;
And so he sallies sternly forth,
Like the cold Genius of the North,
To check the heart's exuberant fulness,
And chill good-humour into dulness.
Where'er he comes, his fellows shrink

* Two constant supporters of that instructive miscellany.

Before his awful nod and wink;
And whensoe'er these features plastic
Assume the savage or sarcastic,
Mirth stands abashed, and Laughter flies,
And Humour faints, and Quibble dies.
How sour he seems!—and, hark! he spoke;
We'll stop and listen to the croak;
'Twill charm us if these happy lays
Are honoured by a fool's dispraise!—
"You think the boats well manned this year!
To you they may perhaps appear!—
I, who have seen those frames of steel,
Tuckfield, and Dixon, and Bulteel,
Can swear,—no matter what I swear!
Only—things are not as they were!
And then our Cricket!—think of that!
We ha'nt a tolerable Bat;
It's very true that Mr. Tucker,
Who puts the Field in such a pucker,
Contrives to make his fifty Runs;—
What then?—we had a Hardinge once!
As for our talents, where are they?
Griffin and Grildrig had their day;
And who's the star of modern time?
Octosyllabic Peregrine;
Who pirates, puns, and talks sedition,
Without a moment's intermission!
And if he did not get a lift,
Sometimes, from me and Doctor Swift,

I can't tell what the deuce he'd do!—
But this, you know, is *entre nous!*
I've tried to talk him into taste,
But found my labour quite misplaced;
He nibs his pen, and twists his ear,
And says he's deaf, and cannot hear;
And if I mention right or rule,—
Egad! he takes me for a fool!"

Gazing upon this varied scene
With a new Artist's absent mien,
I see thee, silent and alone,
My friend, ingenious Hamilton.
I see thee there—(nay, do not blush)—
Knight of the Pallette and the Brush,
Dreaming of straight and crooked lines,
And planning portraits and designs.

I like him hugely!—well I wis
No despicable skill is his,
Whether his sportive canvas shows
Arabia's sands, or Zembla's snows,
A lion, or a bed of lilies,
Fair Caroline, or fierce Achilles;
I love to see him taking down
A school-fellow's unconscious frown,
Describing twist, grimace, contortion,
In most becoming disproportion,
While o'er his merry paper glide

Rivers of wit; and by his side
Caricatura takes her stand,
Inspires the thought, and guides the hand;
I love to see his honoured books
Adorned with rivulets and brooks;
Troy, frowning with her ancient towers,
Or Ida, gay with fruits and flowers;
I love to see fantastic shapes,
Dragons and Griffins, Birds and Apes,
And Pigmy Forms, and Forms Gigantic,
Forms Natural, and Forms Romantic,
Of Dwarfs and Ogres, Dames and Knights,
Scrawled by the side of Homer's fights,
And portraits daubed on Maro's poems,
And profiles pinned to Tully's proems;
In short, I view with partial eyes
Whate'er my brother-painter tries.
To each belongs his own utensil,
I sketch with pen, as he with pencil;
And each, with pencil or with pen,
Hits off a likeness now and then.
He drew *me* once—the spiteful creature!
'Twas voted "like" in every feature;
It might have been so!—('twas lopsided,
And squinted worse than ever I did.)
However, from that hapless day
I owed the debt, which here I pay;
And now I'll give my friend a hint:—
"Unless you want to shine in print,

Paint lords and ladies, nymphs and fairies,
And demi-gods, and dromedaries;
But never be an author's creditor,
Nor paint the picture of an editor!"

Who is the youth with stare confounded,
And tender arms so neatly rounded;
And moveless eyes, and glowing face,
And attitude of studied grace?
Now, Venus, pour your lustre o'er us!
Your would-be servant stands before us.
Hail, Corydon! let others blame
The fury of his fictioned flame;
I love to hear the beardless youth
Talking of constancy and truth;
Swearing more darts are in his liver
Than ever gleamed in Cupid's quiver;
And wondering at those hearts of stone,
Which never melted like his own.
Oh! when I look on Fashion's moth,
Rapt in his visions, and his cloth,
I would not, for a nation's gold,
Disturb the dream, or spoil the fold!

And who the maid whose gilded chain
Hath bound the heart of such a swain?
Ah! look on those surrounding Graces!
There is no lack of pretty faces;
M———l, the Goddess of the night,

Looks beautiful with all her might;
And M———, in that simple dress,
Inthralls us more, by studying less;
D———, in your becoming pride,
Ye march to conquest side by side,
And A——, thou fleetest by,
Bright in thine arch simplicity;
Slight are the links thy power hath wreathed,
Yet, by the tone thy voice hath breathed,
By thy glad smile, and ringlets curled,
I would not break them for the world!
But this is idle! Paying court
I know was never yet my *forte;*
And all I say of Nymph and Queen,
To cut it short, can only mean,
That when I throw my gaze around,
I see much beauty on the ground.

Hark! hark! a mellowed note
Over the water seemed to float!
Hark! the note repeated!
A sweet, and soft, and soothing strain
Echoed, and died, and rose again,
As if the Nymphs of Fairy reign
Were holding to-night their revel rout,
And pouring their fragrant voices out,
On the blue waters seated.
Hark to the tremulous tones that flow,
And the voice of the boatmen as they row!

Cheerfully to the heart they go,
  And touch a thousand pleasant strings
Of Triumph, and Pride, and Hope, and Joy,
And thoughts that are only known to Boy,
  And young Imaginings!
The note is near, the Voice comes clear,
And we catch its Echo on the ear
  With a feeling of delight;
And as the gladdening sounds we hear,
There's many an eager listener here,
  And many a st aining sight.

  One moment,—and ye see
Where, fluttering quick, as the breezes blow,
Backwards and forwards, to and fro,
Bright with the beam of retiring day,
Old Eton's flag on its watery way
  Moves on triumphantly;
But what, that ancient poets have told
Of Amphitrite's Car of Gold,
With the Nymphs behind, and the Nymphs before,
And the Nereid's song, and the Triton's roar,
  Could equal half the pride
That heralds the Monarch's plashing oar
  Over the swelling tide?
And, look!—they land, those gallant crews,
With their jackets light, and their bellying trews;

And Ashley walks, applauded, by,
With a world's talent in his eye;
And Kinglake, dear to Poetry,
  And dearer to his friends;
Hibernian Roberts, you are there,
With that unthinking, merry stare,
  Which still its influence lends
To make us drown our Devils blue,
In laughing at ourselves—and you!
Still I could lengthen out the tale,
And sing Sir Thomas with his ale,
  To all that like to read;
Still I could choose to linger long,
Where Friendship bids the willing song
  Flow out for honest Meade!

Yet, e'en on this triumphant day,
  One thought of grief will rise;
And though I bid my fancy play,
And jest and laugh through all the lay,
Yet sadness still will have its way,
  And burst the vain disguise!
Yes! when the pageant shall have passed,
I shall have look'd upon my last;
I shall not e'er behold again
Our pullers' unremitted strain;
Nor listen to the charming cry
Of contest or of victory,
That speaks what those young bosoms feel,

As keel is pressing fast on keel;
Oh! bright these glories still shall be,
But they shall never dawn for me.
E'en when a Realm's Congratulation
Sang Pæans for the Coronation;
Amidst the pleasure that was round me,
A melancholy Spirit found me;
And while all else were singing "Io!"
I couldn't speak a word but "Heigh ho!"
And so, instead of laughing gayly,
I dropped a tear, and wrote my "VALE."

VALE.

ETON! the Monarch of thy prayers
E'en now receives his load of cares;
Throned in the consecrated choir,
He takes the sceptre of his sire,
And wears the crown his father bore,
And swears the oath his father swore;
And therefore sounds of joy resound,
Fair Eton! on thy classic ground.
A gladder gale is round thee breathed,
And on thy mansions thou hast wreathed
A thousand lamps, whose various hue
Waits but the night to burst to view;
Woe to the poets that refuse
To wake and woo their idle Muse,
When those glad notes—"God save the King,"
From hill, and vale, and hamlet ring!

Hark, how the loved, inspiring tune
Peals forth from every loyal loon
Who loves his country, and excels
In drinking beer, or ringing bells!
It is a day of shouts and greeting,
A day of idleness and eating;
And triumph swells in every soul,
And mighty beeves are roasted whole;
And ale, unbought, is set a-running,
And Pleasure's hymn grows rather stunning;
And children roll upon the green,
And cry—"Confusion to the Queen!"
And Sorrow flies, and Labour slumbers,
And Clio pours her loudest numbers;
And hundreds of that joyous throng,
With whom my life had lingered long,
Give their gay raptures to the gale
In one united, echoing—"Hail!"

I took the harp, I smote the string,
I strove to soar on Fancy's wing;
And murmur in my Sovereign's praise
The latest of my boyhood's lays.
Alas! the theme was too divine
To suit so weak a Muse as mine;
I saw, I felt it could not be;
No song of triumph flows from me:
The harp from which those sounds ye ask
Is all unfit for such a task;

And the last echo of its tone,
Dear Eton, must be thine alone!

A few short hours, and I am borne
Far from the fetters I have worn;
A few short hours, and I am free!—
And yet I shrink from liberty,
And look, and long to give my soul
Back to thy cherishing control.
Control! ah, no! thy chain was meant
Far less for bond than ornament;
And though its links be firmly set,
I never found them gall me yet.
Oh! still through many checkered years,
Mid anxious toils, and hopes, and fears,
Still I have doted on thy fame,
And only gloried in thy name.
How I have loved thee! Thou hast been
My hope, my mistress, and my Queen;
I always found thee kind, and thou
Hast never seen me weep—till now.
I knew that Time was fleeting fast,
I knew thy pleasures could not last,
I knew too well that riper age
Must step upon a busier stage;
Yet when around thine ancient towers
I passed secure my tranquil hours,
Or heard beneath thine aged trees
The drowsy humming of the bees,

Or wandered by thy winding stream,
I would not check my fancy's dream;
Glad in my transitory bliss,
I recked not of an hour like this;
And now the truth comes swiftly on,
The truth I would not think upon;
The last sad thought, so oft delayed,—
"These joys are only born to fade."

Ye Guardians of my earliest days!
Ye Patrons of my earliest lays!
Custom reminds me that to you
Thanks and farewell to-day are due.
Thanks and farewell I give you,—not
(As some that leave this holy spot)
In laboured phrase, and polished lie,
Wrought by the forge of flattery,
But with a heart that cannot tell
The half of what it feels so well.
If I am backward to express,
Believe my love is not the less;
Be kind as you are wont, and view
A thousand thanks in one "Adieu!"
My future life shall strive to show
I wish to pay the debt I owe;
The labours that ye give to May,
September's fruits shall best repay.

And you, my friends, who loved to share
Whate'er was mine of sport or care;

Antagonists at Fives or Chess,
Friends in the Play-ground or the Press,
I leave ye now, and all that rests
Of mutual tastes, and loving breasts,
Is the lone vision, that shall come,
Where'er my studies and my home,
To cheer my labour and my pain,
And make me feel a boy again.

Yes! when at last I sit me down,
A scholar, in my cap and gown,—
When learnèd Doctrines, dark and deep,
Move me to passion or to sleep,—
When Clio yields to Logic's wrangles,
And Long and Short give place to Angles,—
When stern Mathesis makes it treason
To like a rhyme, or scorn a reason,—
With aching head, and weary wit,
Your parted friend shall often sit,
Till Fancy's magic spell hath bound him,
And lonely musings flit around him;
Then shall ye come, with all your wiles
Of gladdening sounds, and warming smiles;
And naught shall meet his eye or ear,
Yet shall he deem your souls are near.

Others may clothe their Valediction
With all the tinsel charms of fiction;
And one may sing of Father Thames,

And Naiads with a hundred names;
And find a Pindus here, and own
The College pump a Helicon;
And search for Gods about the College,
Of which old Homer had no knowledge.
And one may eloquently tell
The triumphs of the Windsor belle,
And sing of Mira's lips and eyes
In oft-repeated ecstasies;
Oh! he hath much and wondrous skill
To paint the looks that wound and kill,
As the poor maid is doomed to brook,
Unconsciously, her lover's look,
And smiles, and talks, until the poet
Hears the band play, and does not know it.
To speak the plain and simple truth,
I always was a jesting youth,
A friend to merriment and fun,
No foe to quibble and to pun;
Therefore I cannot feign a tear;
And, now that I have uttered here
A few unrounded accents, bred
More from the heart than from the head,
Honestly felt, and plainly told,
My lyre is still, my fancy cold.

POEMS OF LIFE AND MANNERS.

PART II.

(Eton, 1826–1832.)

EVERY-DAY CHARACTERS.

I.—THE VICAR.

Some years ago, ere Time and Taste
  Had turned our parish topsy-turvy,
When Darnel Park was Darnel Waste,
  And roads as little known as scurvy,
The man who lost his way between
  St. Mary's Hill and Sandy Thicket,
Was always shown across the Green,
  And guided to the Parson's wicket.

Back flew the bolt of lissom lath;
  Fair Margaret, in her tidy kirtle,
Led the lorn traveller up the path,
  Through clean-clipped rows of box and myrtle;
And Don and Sancho, Tramp and Tray,
  Upon the parlour steps collected,
Wagged all their tails, and seemed to say,
  "Our master knows you; you're expected!"

Up rose the Reverend Doctor Brown,
  Up rose the Doctor's winsome marrow,

The lady laid her knitting down,
  Her husband clasped his ponderous Barrow;
Whate'er the stranger's caste or creed,
  Pundit or papist, saint or sinner,
He found a stable for his steed,
  And welcome for himself, and dinner.

If, when he reached his journey's end,
  And warmed himself in court or college,
He had not gained an honest friend,
  And twenty curious scraps of knowledge;—
If he departed as he came,
  With no new light on love or liquor,—
Good sooth, the traveller was to blame,
  And not the Vicarage, nor the Vicar.

His talk was like a stream which runs
  With rapid change from rocks to roses:
It slipped from politics to puns;
  It passed from Mahomet to Moses;
Beginning with the laws which keep
  The planets in their radiant courses,
And ending with some precept deep
  For dressing eels or shoeing horses.

He was a shrewd and sound divine,
  Of loud Dissent the mortal terror;
And when, by dint of page and line,
  He 'stablished Truth, or started Error,

The Baptist found him far too deep;
  The Deist sighed with saving sorrow;
And the lean Levite went to sleep,
  And dreamed of tasting pork to-morrow.

His sermon never said or showed
  That Earth is foul, that Heaven is gracious,
Without refreshment on the road
  From Jerome, or from Athanasius;
And sure a righteous zeal inspired
  The hand and head that penned and planned
For all who understood, admired, [them,
  And some who did not understand them.

He wrote, too, in a quiet way,
  Small treatises, and smaller verses;
And sage remarks on chalk and clay,
  And hints to noble lords and nurses;
True histories of last year's ghost,
  Lines to a ringlet or a turban;
And trifles to the Morning Post,
  And nothings for Sylvanus Urban.

He did not think all mischief fair,
  Although he had a knack of joking;
He did not make himself a bear,
  Although he had a taste for smoking:
And when religious sects ran mad,
  He held, in spite of all his learning,

That if a man's belief is bad,
  It will not be improved by burning.

And he was kind, and loved to sit
  In the low hut or garnished cottage,
And praise the farmer's homely wit,
  And share the widow's homelier pottage:
At his approach complaint grew mild,
  And when his hand unbarred the shutter,
The clammy lips of Fever smiled
  The welcome which they could not utter.

He always had a tale for me
  Of Julius Cæsar or of Venus:
From him I learned the rule of three,
  Cat's-cradle, leap-frog, and *Quæ genus;*
I used to singe his powdered wig,
  To steal the staff he put such trust in;
And make the puppy dance a jig
  When he began to quote Augustine.

Alack the change! in vain I look
  For haunts in which my boyhood trifled;
The level lawn, the trickling brook,
  The trees I climbed, the beds I rifled:
The church is larger than before;
  You reach it by a carriage entry:
It holds three hundred people more:
  And pews are fitted up for gentry.

Sit in the Vicar's seat: you'll hear
  The doctrine of a gentle Johnian,
Whose hand is white, whose tone is clear,
  Whose phrase is very Ciceronian.
Where is the old man laid?—look down,
  And construe on the slab before you,
HIC JACET GVLIELMVS BROWN,
  VIR NULLA NON DONANDUS LAURA.

(1829.)

II.—QUINCE.

"Fallentis semita vitæ."—*Horace.*

NEAR a small village in the West,
  Where many very worthy people
Eat, drink, play whist, and do their best
  To guard from evil Church and Steeple,
There stood—alas! it stands no more!
  A tenement of brick and plaster,
Of which, for forty years and four,
  My good friend Quince was lord and master!

Welcome was he in hut and hall,
  To maids and matrons, peers and peasants,

He won the sympathies of all,
  By making puns and making presents;
Though all the parish were at strife,
  He kept his counsel and his carriage,
And laughed, and loved a quiet life,
  And shrank from Chancery suits and—marriage.

Sound was his claret and his head;
  Warm was his double ale—and feelings;
His partners at the whist-club said,
  That he was faultless in his dealings.
He went to church but once a week;
  Yet Dr. Poundtext always found him
An upright man, who studied Greek,
  And liked to see his friends around him.

Asylums, hospitals, and schools,
  He used to swear were made to cozen;
All who subscribed to them were fools,
  And he subscribed to half a dozen;
It was his doctrine that the poor
  Were always able, never willing;
And so the beggar at his door
  Had first abuse, and then a shilling.

Some public principles he had,
  But was no flatterer, nor fretter;
He rapped his box when things were bad,

And said, "I cannot make them better!"
And much he loathed the patriot's snort,
And much he scorned the placeman's snuffle,
And cut the fiercest quarrels short,
With—"Patience, gentlemen, and shuffle."

For full ten years his pointer, Speed,
Had couched beneath her master's table;
For twice ten years his old white steed
Had fattened in his master's stable—
Old Quince averred, upon his troth,
They were the ugliest beasts in Devon;
And none knew why he fed them both,
With his own hands, six days in seven.

Whene'er they heard his ring or knock,
Quicker than thought, the village slatterns
Flung down the novel, smoothed the frock,
And took up Mrs. Glasse, and patterns;
Adine was studying baker's bills;
Louisa looked the queen of knitters;
Jane happened to be hemming frills;
And Bell, by chance, was making fritters.

But all was vain; and while decay
Came like a tranquil moonlight o'er him,
And found him gouty still, and gay,
With no fair nurse to bless or bore him;
His rugged smile, and easy chair,

His dread of matrimonial lectures,
His wig, his stick, his powdered hair,
Were themes for very strange conjectures.

Some sages thought the stars above
Had crazed him with excess of knowledge;
Some heard he had been crossed in love,
Before he came away from college—
Some darkly hinted that his Grace
Did nothing, great or small, without him;
Some whispered, with a solemn face,
That there was something odd about him!

I found him at threescore and ten,
A single man, but bent quite double;
Sickness was coming on him then,
To take him from a world of trouble—
He prosed of slipping down the hill,
Discovered he grew older daily;
One frosty day he made his will—
The next he sent for Dr. Bailey!

And so he lived—and so he died:—
When last I sat beside his pillow,
He shook my hand, and "Ah!" he cried,
"Penelope must wear the willow.
Tell her I hugged her rosy chain
While life was flickering in the socket;
And say, that when I call again,
I'll bring a license in my pocket.

"I've left my house and grounds to Fag—
  (I hope his master's shoes will suit him);
And I've bequeathed to you my nag,
  To feed him for my sake—or shoot him.
The Vicar's wife will take old Fox—
  She'll find him an uncommon mouser;
And let her husband have my box,
  My Bible, and my Assmanshauser.

"Whether I ought to die or not
  My doctors cannot quite determine;
It's only clear that I shall rot,
  And be, like Priam, food for vermin.
My debts are paid;—but Nature's debt
  Almost escaped my recollection!
Tom! we shall meet again; and yet
  I cannot leave you my direction!"

III.—THE BELLE OF THE BALL-ROOM.

Years, years ago, ere yet my dreams
  Had been of being wise or witty;
Ere I had done with writing themes,
  Or yawn'd o'er this infernal Chitty;
Years, years ago, while all my joys
  Were in my fowling-piece and filly;

In short, while I was yet a boy,
  I fell in love with Laura Lilly.

I saw her at the County Ball:
  There, when the sounds of flute and fiddle
Gave signal sweet in that old hall,
  Of hands across and down the middle,
Hers was the subtlest spell by far
  Of all that sets young hearts romancing:
She was our queen, our rose, our star;
  And then she danced—oh, heaven, her dancing!

Dark was her hair, her hand was white;
  Her voice was exquisitely tender;
Her eyes were full of liquid light;
  I never saw a waist so slender;
Her every look, her every smile,
  Shot right and left a score of arrows;
I thought 'twas Venus from her isle,
  And wondered where she'd left her sparrows.

She talked of politics or prayers—
  Of Southey's prose, or Wordsworth's sonnets,
Of danglers or of dancing bears,
  Of battles, or the last new bonnets;
By candle-light, at twelve o'clock,
  To me it mattered not a tittle,
If those bright lips had quoted Locke,
  I might have thought they murmured Little.

Through sunny May, through sultry June,
  I loved her with a love eternal;
I spoke her praises to the moon,
  I wrote them to the Sunday Journal.
My mother laughed; I soon found out
  That ancient ladies have no feeling;
My father frown'd; but how should gout
  See any happiness in kneeling?

She was the daughter of a dean,
  Rich, fat, and rather apoplectic;
She had one brother, just thirteen,
  Whose colour was extremely hectic;
Her grandmother, for many a year,
  Had fed the parish with her bounty;
Her second cousin was a peer,
  And lord-lieutenant of the county.

But titles and the three per cents,
  And mortgages, and great relations,
And India bonds, and tithes and rents,
  Oh! what are they to love's sensations?
Black eyes, fair forehead, clustering locks,
  Such wealth, such honours, Cupid chooses;
He cares as little for the stocks,
  As Baron Rothschild for the muses.

She sketched; the vale, the wood, the beach,
  Grew lovelier from her pencil's shading;

She botanized; I envied each
  Young blossom in her boudoir fading;
She warbled Handel; it was grand—
  She made the Catalina jealous;
She touched the organ; I could stand
  For hours and hours to blow the bellows.

She kept an album, too, at home,
  Well filled with all an album's glories;
Paintings of butterflies and Rome,
  Patterns for trimmings, Persian stories;
Soft songs to Julia's cockatoo,
  Fierce odes to famine and to slaughter;
And autographs of Prince Lèboo,
  And recipes of elder water.

And she was flattered, worshipped, bored,
  Her steps were watched, her dress was noted,
Her poodle dog was quite adored,
  Her sayings were extremely quoted.
She laughed, and every heart was glad,
  As if the taxes were abolished;
She frowned, and every look was sad,
  As if the opera were demolished.

She smiled on many just for fun—
  I knew that there was nothing in it;
I was the first, the only one
  Her heart had thought of for a minute;

I knew it, for she told me so,
  In phrase which was divinely moulded;
She wrote a charming hand, and oh!
  How sweetly all her notes were folded!

Our love was like most other loves—
  A little glow, a little shiver;
A rosebud and a pair of gloves,
  And "Fly Not Yet," upon the river;
Some jealousy of some one's heir,
  Some hopes of dying broken-hearted,
A miniature, a lock of hair,
  The usual vows—and then we parted.

We parted—months and years rolled by;
  We met again four summers after;
Our parting was all sob and sigh—
  Our meeting was all mirth and laughter;
For in my heart's most secret cell,
  There had been many other lodgers;
And she was not the ball-room's belle,
  But only—Mrs. Something Rogers!

(1830.)

IV.—MY PARTNER.

"There is, perhaps, no subject of more universal interest in the whole range of natural knowledge, than that of the unceasing fluctuations which take place in the atmosphere in which we are immersed."—*British Almanac.*

At Cheltenham, where one drinks one's fill
Of folly and cold water,
I danced, last year, my first quadrille,
With old Sir Geoffrey's daughter.
Her cheek with summer's rose might vie,
When summer's rose is newest;
Her eyes were blue as autumn's sky,
When autumn's sky is bluest;
And well my heart might deem her one
Of life's most precious flowers,
For half her thoughts were of its sun,
And half were of its showers.

I spoke of novels:—"Vivian Grey"
Was positively charming,
And "Almack's" infinitely gay,
And "Frankenstein" alarming;
I said "De Vere" was chastely told,
Thought well of "Herbert Lacy,"
Called Mr. Banim's sketches "bold,"
And Lady Morgan's "racy;"

I vowed that last new thing of Hook's
  Was vastly entertaining;
And Laura said—"I dote on books,
  Because it's always raining!"

I talked of music's gorgeous fane,
  I raved about Rossini,
Hoped Ronzi would come back again,
  And criticised Pacini;
I wished the chorus singers dumb,
  The trumpets more pacific,
And eulogized Brocard's *à plomb*,
  And voted Paul "terrific!"
What cared she for Medea's pride
  Or Desdemona's sorrow?
"Alas!" my beauteous listener sighed,
  "We must have rain to-morrow!"

I told her tales of other lands;
  Of ever-boiling fountains,
Of poisonous lakes, and barren sands,
  Vast forests, trackless mountains:
I painted bright Italian skies,
  I lauded Persian Roses,
Coined similes for Spanish eyes,
  And jests for Indian noses:
I laughed at Lisbon's love of mass,
  Vienna's dread of treason;
And Laura asked me where the glass
  Stood at Madrid last season.

I broached whate'er had gone its rounds,
  The week before, of scandal;
What made Sir Luke lay down his hounds,
  And Jane take up her Handel;
Why Julia walked upon the heath,
  With the pale moon above her;
Where Flora lost her false front teeth,
  And Anne her falser lover;
How Lord de B. and Mrs. L.
  Had crossed the sea together;
My shuddering partner cried—"*O Ciel!*
  How could they—in such weather?"

Was she a Blue?—I put my trust
  In strata, petals, gases;
A boudoir pedant?—I discussed
  The toga and the fasces;
A cockney-muse?—I mouthed a deal
  Of folly from "Endymion;"
A saint?—I praised the pious zeal
  Of Messrs. Way and Simeon;
A politician?—It was vain
  To quote the morning paper;
The horrid phantoms came again,
  Rain, hail, and snow, and vapor.

Flat flattery was my only chance:
  I acted deep devotion,
Found magic in her every glance,

Grace in her every motion;
I wasted all a stripling's lore,
Prayer, passion, folly, feeling,
And wildly looked upon the floor,
And wildly on the ceiling;
I envied gloves upon her arm,
And shawls upon her shoulder;
And when my worship was most warm,
She "never found it colder."

I don't object to wealth or land;
And she will have the giving
Of an extremely pretty hand,
Some thousands, and a living.
She makes silk purses, broiders stools,
Sings sweetly, dances finely,
Paints screens, subscribes to Sunday schools,
And sits a horse divinely.
But to be linked for life to her!
The desperate man who tried it,
Might marry a Barometer,
And hang himself beside it!

(1828.)

V.—PORTRAIT OF A LADY.

IN THE EXHIBITION OF THE ROYAL ACADEMY.

WHAT are you, Lady?—naught is here
  To tell us of your name or story;
To claim the gazer's smile or tear,
  To dub you Whig, or damn your Tory.
It is beyond a poet's skill
  To form the slightest notion, whether
We e'er shall walk through one quadrille,
  Or look upon one moon together.

You're very pretty!—all the world
  Are talking of your bright brow's splendour,
And of your locks, so softly curled,
  And of your hands, so white and slender·
Some think you're blooming in Bengal;
  Some say you're blowing in the city;
Some know you're nobody at all;
  I only feel, you're very pretty.

But bless my heart! it's very wrong:
  You're making all our belles ferocious;
Anne "never saw a chin so long;"
  And Laura thinks your dress "atrocious;"

And Lady Jane, who now and then
  Is taken for the village steeple,
Is sure you can't be four feet ten,
  And " wonders at the taste of people."

Soon pass the praises of a face;
  Swift fades the very best vermilion;
Fame rides a most prodigious pace;
  Oblivion follows on the pillion;
And all who, in these sultry rooms,
  To-day have stared, and pushed, and fainted,
Will soon forget your pearls and plumes,
  As if they never had been painted.

You'll be forgotten—as old debts
  By persons who are used to borrow;
Forgotten—as the sun that sets,
  When shines a new one on the morrow;
Forgotten—like the luscious peach,
  That blessed the school-boy last September;
Forgotten—like a maiden speech,
  Which all men praise, but none remember.

Yet, ere you sink into the stream,
  That whelms alike sage, saint, and martyr,
And soldier's sword, and minstrel's theme,
  And Canning's wit, and Gatton's charter,
Here of the fortunes of your youth
  My fancy weaves her dim conjectures,

Which have, perhaps, as much of truth
  As Passion's vows, or Cobbett's lectures.

Was't in the north or in the south,
  That summer-breezes rocked your cradle?
And had you in your baby mouth
  A wooden or a silver ladle?
And was your first, unconscious sleep,
  By brownie banned, or blessed by fairy?
And did you wake to laugh or weep?
  And were you christened Maud or Mary?

And was your father called "your grace?"
  And did he bet at Ascot races?
And did he chat at common-place?
  And did he fill a score of places?
And did your lady-mother's charms
  Consist in picklings, broilings, bastings?
Or did she prate about the arms
  Her brave forefathers wore at Hastings?

Where were you "finished?" tell me where!
  Was it at Chelsea, or at Chiswick?
Had you the ordinary share
  Of books and backboard, harp and physic?
And did they bid you banish pride,
  And mind your oriental tinting?
And did you learn how Dido died,
  And who found out the art of printing?

And are you fond of lanes and brooks,
  A votary of the sylvan muses?
Or do you con the little books
  Which Baron Brougham and Vaux diffuses?
Or do you love to knit and sew,
  The fashionable world's Arachne?
Or do you canter down the Row,
  Upon a very long-tailed hackney?

And do you love your brother James?
  And do you pet his mares and setters?
And have your friends romantic names?
  And do you write them long, long letters?
And are you—since the world began
  All women are—a little spiteful?
And don't you dote on Malibran?
  And don't you think Tom Moore delightful?

I see they've brought you flowers to-day,
  Delicious food for eyes and noses;
But carelessly you turn away
  From all the pinks, and all the roses;
Say, is that fond look sent in search
  Of one whose look as fondly answers?
And is he, fairest, in the Church,
  Or is he—ain't he—in the Lancers?

And is your love a motley page
  Of black and white, half joy, half sorrow?

Are you to wait till you're of age?
  Or are you to be his to-morrow?
Or do they bid you, in their scorn,
  Your pure and sinless flame to smother?
Is he so very meanly born?
  Or are you married to another?

Whate'er you are, at last, adieu!
  I think it is your bounden duty
To let the rhymes I coin for you,
  Be prized by all who prize your beauty.
From you I seek nor gold nor fame;
  From you I fear no cruel strictures;
I wish some girls that I could name
  Were half as silent as their pictures!

(1831.)

THE CHILDE'S DESTINY.

"And none did love him—not his lemans dear."—*Byron.*

No mistress of the hidden skill,
  No wizard gaunt and grim,
Went up by night to heath or hill
  To read the stars for him;
The merriest girl in all the land
  Of vine-encircled France

Bestowed upon his brow and hand
  Her philosophic glance:
"I bind thee with a spell," said she,
  "I sign thee with a sign;
No woman's love shall light on thee,
  No woman's heart be thine!

"And trust me, 'tis not that thy cheek
  Is colourless and cold;
Nor that thine eye is slow to speak
  What only eyes have told;
For many a cheek of paler white
  Hath blushed with passion's kiss,
And many an eye of lesser light
  Hath caught its fire from bliss;
Yet while the rivers seek the sea,
  And while the young stars shine,
No woman's love shall light on thee,—
  No woman's heart be thine!

"And 'tis not that thy spirit, awed
  By Beauty's numbing spell,
Shrinks from the force or from the fraud
  Which Beauty loves so well;
For thou hast learned to watch, and wake,
  And swear by earth and sky;
And thou art very bold to take
  What we must still deny:
I cannot tell;—the charm was wrought

By other threads than mine;
The lips are lightly begged or bought,—
The heart may not be thine!

"Yet thine the brightest smiles shall be
That ever Beauty wore;
And confidence from two or three,
And compliments from more;
And one shall give—perchance hath given—
What only is not love,—
Friendship,—oh! such as saints in Heaven
Rain on us from above:
If she shall meet thee in the bower,
Or name thee in the shrine,
O wear the ring and guard the flower!
Her heart may not be thine!

"Go, set thy boat before the blast,
Thy breast before the gun;
The haven shall be reached at last,
The battle shall be won:
Or muse upon thy country's laws,
Or strike thy country's lute;
And patriot hands shall sound applause,
And lovely lips be mute.
Go, dig the diamond from the wave,
The treasure from the mine;
Enjoy the wreath, the gold, the grave,—
No woman's heart is thine!

"I charm thee from the agony
  Which others feel or feign;
From anger, and from jealousy,
  From doubt, and from disdain;
I bid thee wear the scorn of years
  Upon the cheek of youth,
And curl the lip at Passion's tears,
  And shake the head at truth:
While there is bliss in revelry,
  Forgetfulness in wine,
Be thou from woman's love as free
  As woman is from thine!"

(1825.)

JOSEPHINE.

We did not meet in courtly hall,
  Where Birth and Beauty throng,
Where Luxury holds festival,
  And wit awakes the song;
We met where darker spirits meet,
  In the home of Sin and Shame,
Where Satan shows his cloven feet,
  And hides his titled name;
And she knew she could not be, Love,
  What once she might have been,
But she was kind to me, Love,
  My pretty Josephine.

We did not part beneath the sky,
  As warmer lovers part,
Where Night conceals the glistening eye,
  But not the throbbing heart;
We parted on the spot of ground
  Where we first had laughed at love,
And ever the jests were loud around,
  And the lamps were bright above:
"The heaven is very dark, Love,
  The blast is very keen,
But merrily rides my bark, Love—
  Good night, my Josephine!"

She did not speak of ring or vow,
  But filled the cup of wine,
And took the roses from her brow
  To make a wreath for mine;
And bade me, when the gale should lift
  My light skiff o'er the wave,
To think as little of the gift
  As of the hand that gave:
"Go gayly o'er the sea, Love,
  And find your own heart's queen;
And look not back to me, Love,
  Your humble Josephine!"

That garland breathes and blooms no more,
  Past are those idle hours;
I would not, could I choose, restore

The fondness or the flowers;
Yet oft their withered witchery
Revives its wonted thrill,
Remembered—not with Passion's sigh,
But, oh! remembered still:
And even from your side, Love,
And even from this scene,
One look is o'er the tide, Love,
One thought with Josephine!

Alas! your lips are rosier,
Your eyes of softer blue,
And I have never felt for her
As I have felt for you;
Our love was like the bright snow-flakes,
Which melt before you pass—
Or the bubble on the wine, which breaks
Before you lip the glass.
You saw these eye-lids wet, Love,
Which she has never seen;
But bid me not forget, Love,
My poor Josephine!

(1826.)

THE CHANT OF THE BRAZEN HEAD.

"Brazen companion of my solitary hours! do you, while I recline, pronounce a prologue to those sentiments of wisdom and virtue, which are hereafter to be the oracles of statesmen and the guides of philosophers. Give me to-night a proem of our essay, an opening of our case, a division of our subject. Speak!"—(*Slow music. The Friar falls asleep. The Head chants as follows.*)—THE BRAZEN HEAD.

"I THINK, whatever mortals crave,
With impotent endeavour,
A wreath—a rank—a throne—a grave—
The world goes round forever;
I think that life is not too long,
And therefore I determine
That many people read a song,
Who will not read a sermon.

"I think you've looked through many hearts,
And mused on many actions,
And studied man's component parts,
And nature's compound fractions;
I think you've picked up truth by bits
From foreigner and neighbour,
I think the world has lost its wits,
And you have lost your labour.

"I think the studies of the wise,
  The hero's noisy quarrel,
The majesty of woman's eyes,
  The poet's cherished laurel;
And all that makes us lean or fat,
  And all that charms or troubles—
This bubble is more bright than that,
  But still they all are bubbles.

"I think the thing you call Renown,
  This unsubstantial vapour
For which a soldier burns a town,
  The sonneteer a taper,
Is like the mist which, as he flies,
  The horseman leaves behind him;
He cannot mark its wreaths arise,
  Or, if he does, they blind him.

"I think one nod of Mistress Chance
  Makes creditors of debtors,
And shifts the funeral for the dance,
  The sceptre for the fetters;
I think that Fortune's favoured guest
  May live to gnaw the platters;
And he that wears the purple vest
  May wear the rags and tatters.

"I think the Tories love to buy
  'Your Lordships' and 'Your Graces,'

By loathing common honesty,
  And lauding common places;
I think that some are very wise,
  And some are very funny,
And some grow rich by telling lies,
  And some by telling money.

"I think the Whigs are wicked knaves,
  And very like the Tories,
Who doubt that Britain rules the waves,
  And ask the price of glories;
I think that many fret and fume
  At what their friends are planning,
And Mr. Hume hates Mr. Brougham
  As much as Mr. Canning.

"I think that friars and their hoods,
  Their doctrines and their maggots,
Have lighted up too many feuds,
  And far too many fagots;
I think while zealots fast and frown,
  And fight for two or seven,
That there are fifty roads to town,
  And rather more to Heaven.

"I think that, thanks to Paget's lance,
  And thanks to Chester's learning,
The hearts that burned for fame in France,
  At home are safe from burning;

I think the Pope is on his back,
  And, though 'tis fun to shake him,
I think the Devil not so black
  As many people make him.

"I think that Love is like a play
  Where tears and smiles are blended,
Or like a faithless April day,
  Whose shine with shower is ended;
Like Colnbrook pavement, rather rough,
  Like trade, exposed to losses,
And like a Highland plaid, all stuff,
  And very full of crosses.

"I think the world, though dark it be,
  Has aye one rapturous pleasure,
Concealed in life's monotony,
  For those who seek the treasure;
One planet in a starless night—
  One blossom on a brier—
One friend not quite a hypocrite—
  One woman not a liar!

"I think poor beggars court St. Giles,
  Rich beggars court St. Stephen;
And death looks down with nods and smiles,
  And makes the odds all even.
I think some die upon the field,
  And some upon the billow,

And some are laid beneath a shield,
  And some beneath a willow.

"I think that very few have sighed,
  When Fate at last has found them,
Though bitter foes were by their side,
  And barren moss around them;
I think that some have died of drought,
  And some have died of drinking;
I think that naught is worth a thought,
  And I'm a fool for thinking."

(1826.)

TWENTY-EIGHT AND TWENTY-NINE.

"Rien n'est changé, mes amis."—*Charles X.*

I HEARD a sick man's dying sigh,
  And an infant's idle laughter,
The Old Year went with mourning by—
  The New came dancing after!
Let Sorrow shed her lonely tear,
  Let Revelry hold her ladle;
Bring boughs of cypress for the bier,
  Fling roses on the cradle;
Mutes to wait on the funeral state;
  Pages to pour the wine;

A requiem for Twenty-Eight,
  And a health to Twenty-Nine!

Alas for human happiness!
  Alas for human sorrow!
Our yesterday is nothingness,
  What else will be our morrow?
Still Beauty must be stealing hearts,
  And Knavery stealing purses;
Still cooks must live by making tarts,
  And wits by making verses;
While sages prate and courts debate,
  The same stars set and shine;
And the world, as it rolled through Twenty-Eight,
  Must roll through Twenty-Nine.

Some King will come, in Heaven's good time,
  To the tomb his father came to;
Some Thief will wade through blood and crime
  To a crown he has no claim to;
Some suffering land will rend in twain
  The manacles that bound her,
And gather the links of the broken chain
  To fasten them proudly round her;
The grand and great will love and hate,
  And combat and combine;
And much where we were in Twenty-Eight,
  We shall be in Twenty-Nine.

O'Connell will toil to raise the Rent,
  And Kenyon to sink the Nation;
And Sheil will abuse the Parliament,
  And Peel the Association;
And the thought of bayonets and swords
  Will make ex-chancellors merry;
And jokes will be cut in the House of Lords,
  And throats in the County Kerry;
And writers of weight will speculate
  On the Cabinet's design;
And just what it did in Twenty-Eight
  It will do in Twenty-Nine.

John Thomas Mugg, on a lonely hill,
  Will do a deed of mystery;
The Morning Chronicle will fill
  Five columns with the history;
The jury will be all surprise,
  The prisoner quite collected,
And Justice Park will wipe his eyes,
  And be very much affected;
And folks will relate poor Corder's fate
  As they hurry home to dine,
Comparing the hangings of Twenty-Eight
  With the hangings of Twenty-Nine.

And the Goddess of Love will keep her smiles,
  And the God of Cups his orgies;
And there'll be riots in St. Giles,

And weddings in St. George's;
And mendicants will sup like Kings,
And Lords will swear like lackeys;
And black eyes oft will lead to rings,
And rings will lead to black eyes;
And pretty Kate will scold her mate,
In a dialect all divine;
Alas! they married in Twenty-Eight,
They will part in Twenty-Nine.

And oh! I shall find how, day by day,
All thoughts and things look older;
How the laugh of Pleasure grows less gay,
And the heart of Friendship colder;
But still I shall be what I have been,
Sworn foe to Lady Reason,
And seldom troubled with the spleen,
And fond of talking treason;
I shall buckle my skate, and leap my gate,
And throw and write my line;
And the woman I worshipped in Twenty-Eight
I shall worship in Twenty-Nine.

(January 1, 1829.)

SONG FOR THE FOURTEENTH OF FEBRUARY.

BY A GENERAL LOVER.

"Mille gravem telis, exhaustâ pene pharetrâ."

Apollo has peeped through the shutter,
  And wakened the witty and fair;
The boarding-school belle's in a flutter,
  The two-penny post's in despair;
The breath of the morning is flinging
  A magic on blossom, on spray,
And cockneys and sparrows are singing
  In chorus on Valentine's Day.

Away with ye, dreams of disaster,
  Away with ye, visions of law,
Of cases I never shall master,
  Of pleadings I never shall draw!
Away with ye, parchments and papers,
  Red tapes, unread volumes, away!
It gives a fond lover the vapours
  To see you on Valentine's Day.

I'll sit in my night-cap, like Hayley,
  I'll sit with my arms crossed like Spain,
Till joys, which are vanishing daily,
  Come back in their lustre again:

Oh! shall I look over the waters,
  Or shall I look over the way,
For the brightest and best of Earth's daughters,
  To rhyme to, on Valentine's Day?

Shall I crown with my worship, for fame's sake,
  Some goddess whom Fashion has starred,
Make puns on Miss Love and her namesake,
  Or pray for a *pas* with Brocard?
Shall I flirt, in romantic idea,
  With Chester's adorable clay,
Or whisper in transport, "*Si mea**
  Cum Vestris"—on Valentine's Day?

Shall I kneel to a Sylvia or Celia,
  Whom no one e'er saw, or may see,
A fancy-drawn Laura Amelia,
  An *ad libit.* Anna Marie?
Shall I court an initial with stars to it,
  Go mad for a G. or a J.,
Get Bishop to put a few bars to it,
  And print it on Valentine's Day?

I think not of Laura the witty;
  For, oh! she is married at York!
I sigh not for Rose of the City,
  For, oh! she is buried at Cork!

* "Si mea cum *vestris* valuissent vota!"—Ovid, *Met.*

Adèle has a braver and better
  To say—what I never could say;
Louise cannot construe a letter
  Of English, on Valentine's Day.

So perish the leaves in the arbour!
  The tree is all bare in the blast;
Like a wreck that is drifting to harbour,
  I come to thee, Lady, at last:
Where art thou, so lovely and lonely?
  Though idle the lute and the lay,
The lute and the lay are thine only,
  My fairest, on Valentine's Day.

For thee I have opened my Blackstone,
  For thee I have shut up myself;
Exchanged my long curls for a Caxton,
  And laid my short whist on the shelf;
For thee I have sold my old sherry,
  For thee I have burned my new play:
And I grow philosophical,—very!
  Except upon Valentine's Day!

(February 14, 1826.)

APRIL FOOLS.

——"passim
Palantes error certo de tramite pellit;
Ille sinistrorsum, hic dextrorsum abit."—*Hor.*

This day, beyond all contradiction,
This day is all thine own, Queen Fiction!
And thou art building castles boundless
Of groundless joys, and griefs as groundless;
Assuring beauties that the border
Of their new dress is out of order;
And schoolboys that their shoes want tying;
And babies that their dolls are dying.
Lend me, lend me some disguise;
I will tell prodigious lies;
All who care for what I say
Shall be Aprll fools to-day.

First, I relate how all the nation
Is ruined by Emancipation;
How honest men are sadly thwarted;
How beads and fagots are imported;
How every parish church looks thinner;
How Peel has asked the Pope to dinner;
And how the Duke, who fought the duel,
Keeps good King George on water-gruel.

Thus I waken doubts and fears
In the Commons and the Peers;
If they care for what I say,
They are April fools to-day.

Next I announce to hall and hovel
Lord Asterisk's unwritten novel.
It's full of wit, and full of fashion,
And full of taste, and full of passion;
It tells some very curious histories,
Elucidates some charming mysteries,
And mingles sketches of society
With precepts of the soundest piety.
Thus I babbled to the host
Who adore the "Morning Post;"
If they care for what I say,
They are April fools to-day.

Then to the artist of my raiment
I hint his bankers have stopped payment;
And just suggest to Lady Locket
That somebody has picked her pocket;
And scare Sir Thomas from the city
By murmuring, in a tone of pity,
That I am sure I saw my Lady
Drive through the Park with Captain Grady.
Off my troubled victims go,
Very pale and very low;
If they care for what I say,
They are April fools to-day.

I've sent the learnèd Doctor Trepan
To feel Sir Hubert's broken kneepan;
'Twill rout the doctor's seven senses
To find Sir Hubert charging fences!
I've sent a sallow parchment scraper
To put Miss Trim's last will on paper;
He'll see her, silent as a mummy,
At whist with her two maids and dummy.
Man of brief, and man of pill,
They will take it very ill;
If they care for what I say,
They are April fools to-day,

And then to her, whose smile shed light on
My weary lot last year at Brighton,
I talk of happiness and marriage,
St. George's, and a travelling carriage.
I trifle with my rosy fetters,
I rave about her witching letters,
And swear my heart shall do no treason
Before the closing of the season.
Thus I whisper in the ear
Of Louisa Windermere;
If she cares for what I say,
She's an April fool to-day.

And to the world I publish gayly
That all things are improving daily;
That suns grow warmer, streamlets clearer,

And faith more warm, and love sincerer;
That children grow extremely clever;
That sin is seldom known, or never;
That gas, and steam, and education,
Are killing sorrow and starvation!
  Pleasant visions,—but, alas!
  How those pleasant visions pass!
  If you care for what I say,
  You're an April fool to-day.

  Last, to myself, when night comes round me,
And the soft chain of thought has bound me,
I whisper, "Sir, your eyes are killing;
You owe no mortal man a shilling;
You never cringe for star or garter,
You're much too wise to be a martyr;
And since you must be food for vermin,
You don't feel much desire for ermine!"
  Wisdom is a mine, no doubt,
  If one can but find it out;
  But, whate'er I think or say,
  I'm an April fool to-day.

(April 1, 1829.)

GOOD-NIGHT TO THE SEASON.

"So runs the world away."—*Hamlet.*

Good-night to the Season! 'tis over!
  Gay dwellings no longer are gay;
The courtier, the gambler, the lover,
  Are scattered like swallows away;
There's nobody left to invite one,
  Except my good uncle and spouse;
My mistress is bathing at Brighton,
  My patron is sailing at Cowes;
For want of a better employment,
  Till Ponto and Don can get out,
I'll cultivate rural enjoyment,
  And angle immensely for trout.

Good-night to the Season! the lobbies,
  Their changes, and rumours of change,
Which startled the rustic Sir Bobbies,
  And made all the Bishops look strange;
The breaches, and battles, and blunders,
  Performed by the Commons and Peers;
The Marquis's eloquent thunders,
  The Baronet's eloquent ears;

Denouncings of Papists and treasons,
  Of foreign dominion, and oats;
Misrepresentations of reasons,
  And misunderstandings of notes.

Good-night to the Season! the building's
  Enough to make Inigo sick;
The paintings, and plasterings, and gildings
  Of stucco, and marble, and brick;
The orders deliciously blended,
  From love of effect, into one;
The club-houses only intended,
  The palaces only begun;
The hell, where the fiend in his glory
  Sits staring at putty and stones,
And scrambles from story to story,
  To rattle at midnight his bones.

Good-night to the Season! the dances,
  The fillings of hot little rooms,
The glancings of rapturous glances,
  The fancyings of fancy costumes;
The pleasures which fashion makes duties
  The praisings of fiddles and flutes,
The luxury of looking at beauties,
  The tedium of talking to mutes;
The female diplomatists, planners
  Of matches for Laura and Jane,
The ice of her Ladyship's manners,
  The ice of his Lordship's champagne.

Good-night to the Season! the rages
  Led off by the chiefs of the throng,
The Lady Matilda's new pages,
  The Lady Eliza's new song;
Miss Fennel's macaw, which at Boodle's
  Was held to have something to say;
Mrs. Splenetic's musical poodles,
  Which bark "Batti—Batti!" all day;
The pony Sir Araby sported,
  As hot and as black as a coal,
And the lion his mother imported,
  In bearskins and grease, from the Pole.

Good-night to the Season! the Toso,
  So very majestic and tall;
Miss Ayton, whose singing was so-so,
  And Pasta, divinest of all;
The labour in vain of the ballet,
  So sadly deficient in stars;
The foreigners thronging the Alley,
  Exhaling the breath of cigars;
The *loge*, where some heiress, how killing!—
  Environed with exquisites, sits,
The lovely one out of her drilling,
  The silly ones out of their wits.

Good-night to the Season! the splendour
  That beamed in the Spanish bazaar,
Where I purchased—my heart was so tender—

A card-case,—a pasteboard guitar,—
A bottle of perfume,—a girdle,—
A lithographed Riego, full-grown,
Whom bigotry drew on a hurdle,
That artists might draw him on stone,—
A small panorama of Seville,—
A trap for demolishing flies,—
A caricature of the Devil,—
And a look from Miss Sheridan's eyes.

Good-night to the Season! the flowers
Of the grand horticultural fête,
When boudoirs were quitted for bowers,
And the fashion was, not to be late;
When all who had money and leisure
Grew rural o'er ices and wines,
All pleasantly toiling for pleasure,
All hungrily pining for pines,
And making of beautiful speeches,
And marring of beautiful shows,
And feeding on delicate peaches,
And treading on delicate toes.

Good-night to the Season! another
Will come with its trifles and toys,
And hurry away, like its brother,
In sunshine, and odour, and noise.
Will it come with a rose, or a brier?
Will it come with a blessing, or curse?

Will its bonnets be lower, or higher?
  Will its morals be better, or worse?
Will it find me grown thinner, or fatter,
  Or fonder of wrong or of right,
Or married, or buried?—no matter,—
  Good-night to the Season!—Good-night!

(AUGUST, 1827.)

ARRIVALS AT A WATERING-PLACE.

I PLAY a spade:—such strange new faces
  Are flocking in from near and far;
Such frights—Miss Dobbs holds all the aces,—
  One can't imagine who they are!
The lodgings at enormous prices,
  New Donkeys, and another fly;
And Madame Bonbon out of ices,
  Although we're scarcely in July:
We're quite as sociable as any,
  But one old horse can hardly crawl;
And really, where there are so many,
  We can't tell where we ought to call.

Pray, who has seen the odd old fellow
  Who took the Doctor's house last week?—

A pretty chariot,—livery yellow—
  Almost as yellow as his cheek:
A widower, sixty-five, and surly—
  And stiffer than a poplar-tree;
Drinks rum and water, gets up early
  To dip his carcass in the sea;
He's always in a monstrous hurry,
  And always talking of Bengal;
They say his cook makes noble curry;—
  I think, Louisa, we should call.

And so Miss Jones, the Mantua-maker,
  Has let her cottage on the hill!—
The drollest man, a sugar-baker,
  Last year imported from the till;
Prates of his "*orses*" and his "*oney*,"
  Is quite in love with fields and farms;
A horrid Vandal,—but his money
  Will buy a glorious coat-of-arms;
Old Clyster makes him take the waters;
  Some say he means to give a ball;
And, after all, with thirteen daughters,
  I think, Sir Thomas, you might call.

That poor young man!—I'm sure and certain
  Despair is making up his shroud;
He walks all night beneath the curtain
  Of the dim sky and murky cloud:
  ...s landscapes, throws such mournful glances!

Writes verses,—has such splendid eyes;—
An ugly name,—but Laura fancies
He's some great person in disguise!—
And since his dress is all the fashion,
And since he's very dark and tall,
I think that, out of pure compassion,
I'll get papa to go and call.

So Lord St. Ives is occupying
The whole of Mr. Ford's Hotel;
Last Saturday his man was trying
A little nag I want to sell.
He brought a lady in the carriage;
Blue eyes,—eighteen,—or thereabouts;—
Of course, you know, we *hope* it's marriage!
But yet the *femme de chambre* doubts.
She looked so pensive when we met her;
Poor thing! and such a charming shawl!—
Well! till we understand it better,
It's quite impossible to call.

Old Mr. Fund, the London banker,
Arrived to-day at Premium Court;
I would not, for the world, cast anchor
In such a horrid, dangerous port;
Such dust and rubbish, lath and plaster
(Contractors play the meanest tricks)—
The roof's as crazy as its master,
And he was born in fifty-six:

Stairs creaking,—cracks in every landing,—
  The colonnade is sure to fall;
We shan't find post or pillar standing,
  Unless we make great haste to call.

Who was that sweetest of sweet creatures,
  Last Sunday, in the Rector's seat?
The finest shape,—the loveliest features,—
  I never saw such tiny feet.
My brother (this is quite between us),
  Poor Arthur,—'twas a sad affair!
Love at first sight,—she's quite a Venus,—
  But then she's poorer far than fair:
And so my father and my mother
  Agreed it would not do at all;
And so,—I'm sorry for my brother!—
  It's settled that we're not to call.

And there's an Author, full of knowledge;
  And there's a Captain on half pay;
And there's a Baronet from College,
  Who keeps a boy, and rides a bay;
And sweet Sir Marcus, from the Shannon,
  Fine specimen of brogue and bone;
And Doctor Calipee, the Canon,
  Who weighs, I fancy, twenty stone;
A maiden lady is adorning
  The faded front of Lily Hall;—
Upon my word, the first fine morning
  We'll make a round, my dear, and call.

Alas! disturb not, maid and matron,
  The swallow in my humble thatch;
Your son may find a better patron,
  Your niece may meet a richer match:
I can't afford to give a dinner,—
  I never was on Almack's list;
And since I seldom rise a winner,
  I never like to play at whist:
Unknown to me the stocks are falling;
  Unwatched by me the glass may fall;
Let all the world pursue its calling,—
  I'm not at home if people call.

(1829.)

THE FANCY BALL.

"A visor for a visor! what care I
What curious eye doth quote deformities?"
Shakspeare.

"You used to talk," said Miss Mac Call,
  "Of flowers, and flames, and Cupid;
But now you never talk at all;
  You're getting vastly stupid.
You'd better burn your Blackstone, Sir,
  You never will get through it;
There's a Fancy Ball at Winchester,
  Do let us take you to it."

I made that night a solemn vow,
  To startle all beholders;
I wore white muslin on my brow,
  Green velvet on my shoulders;
My trousers were supremely wide,
  I learned to swear "by Allah!"
I stuck a poniard by my side,
  And called myself "Abdallah!"

Oh! a Fancy Ball's a strange affair,
  Made up of silks and leathers,
Light heads, light heels, false hearts, false hair,
  Pins, paint, and ostrich-feathers;
The dullest Duke in all the town
  To-day may shine a droll one;
And rakes, who have not half a crown,
  Look royal in a whole one.

Go, call the lawyer from his pleas,
  The school-boy from his Latin;
Be stoics here in ecstasies,
  And savages in satin;
Let young and old forego—forget
  Their labour and their sorrow,
And none—except the Cabinet—
  Take counsel for the morrow.

Begone, dull care! This life of ours
  Is very dark and chilly;

We'll sleep through all its serious hours,
  And laugh through all its silly.
Be mine such motley scene as this,
  Where, by established usance,
Miss Gravity is quite amiss,
  And Madam Sense a nuisance!

Hail, blest Confusion! here are met
  All tongues, and times, and faces;
The Lancers flirt with Juliet,
  The Brahmin talks of races;
And where's your genius, bright Corinne?
  And where your brogue, Sir Lucius?
And, Chinca Ti, you have not seen
  One chapter of Confucius.

Lo! dandies from Kamtschatka flirt
  With beauties from the Wrekin;
And belles from Berne look very pert
  On Mandarins from Pekin;
The Cardinal is here from Rome,
  The Commandant from Seville,
And Hamlet's father from the tomb,
  And Faustus from the Devil.

O sweet Anne Page!—those dancing eyes
  Have peril in their splendour!
"O sweet Anne Page!"—so Slender sighs,
  And what am I, but slender?
Alas! when next your spells engage

So fond and starved a sinner,
My pretty Page, be Shakspeare's Page,
And ask the fool to dinner!

What mean those laughing Nuns, I pray,
What mean they, Nun or Fairy?
I guess they told no beads to-day,
And sang no Ave Mary;
From Mass and Matins, Priest and Pix,
Barred door, and window grated,
I wish all pretty Catholics
Were thus emancipated.

Four Seasons come to dance quadrilles
With four well-seasoned sailors;
And Raleigh talks of railroad bills
With Timon, prince of railers;
I find Sir Charles, of Aubyn Park,
Equipped for a walk to Mecca;
And I run away from Joan of Arc,
To romp with sad Rebecca.

Fair Cleopatra's very plain,
Puck halts, and Ariel swaggers;
And Cæsar's murdered o'er again,
Though not by Roman daggers;
Great Charlemagne is four feet high,
Sad stuff has Bacon spoken,
Queen Mary's waist is all awry,
And Psyche's nose is broken.

Our happiest bride,—how very odd!—
  Is the mourning Isabella;
And the heaviest foot that ever trod
  Is the foot of Cinderella;
Here sad Calista laughs outright,
  There Yorick looks most grave, Sir,
And a Templar waves the cross to-night,
  Who never crossed the wave, Sir.

And what a Babel is the talk!
  "The Giraffe"—"plays the fiddle"—
"Macadam's roads"—"I hate this chalk"—
  "Sweet girl!"—"a charming riddle"—
"I'm nearly drunk with"—"Epsom salts"—
  "Yes, separate beds"—"such cronies!"—
"Good Heaven! who taught that man to waltz?"
  "A pair of Shetland ponies."

"Lord Nugent"—"an enchanting shape"—
  "Will move for"—"Maraschino;"—
"Pray, Julia, how's your mother's ape?"—
  "He died at Navarino!"—
"The gout, by Jove, is"—"apple pie;"—
  "Don Miguel"—"Tom the Tinker;"—
"His Lordship's pedigree's as high
  As"—"Whipcord, dam by Clinker."

"Love's shafts are weak"—"my chestnut kicks"—

"Heart-broken"—"broke the traces;"—
"What say you now of politics?"—
"Change sides, and to your places!"—
"A five-barred gate"—"a precious pearl"—
"Grave things may all be punned on!"—
"The Whigs, thank Heaven, are"—"out of curl"—
"Her age is"—"four by London!"

Thus run the giddy hours away,
Till morning's light is beaming,
And we must go to dream by day
All we to-night are dreaming;
To smile and sigh, to love and change,
Oh! in our heart's recesses,
We dress in fancies quite as strange
As these, our fancy-dresses.

(1828.)

A LETTER OF ADVICE.

FROM MISS MEDORA TREVILIAN, AT PADUA, TO MISS ARAMINTA VAVASOUR, IN LONDON.

"Enfin Monsieur, un homme aimable;
Voilà pourquoi je ne saurais l'aimer."—*Scribe.*

You tell me you're promised a lover,
  My own Araminta, next week;
Why cannot my fancy discover
  The hue of his coat, and his cheek?
Alas! if he look like another,
  A vicar, a banker, a beau,
Be deaf to your father and mother,
  My own Araminta, say "No!"

Miss Lane, at her Temple of Fashion,
  Taught us both how to sing and to speak,
And we loved one another with passion
  Before we had been there a week;
You gave me a ring for a token,
  I wear it wherever I go;
I gave you a chain—is it broken?
  My own Araminta, say "No!"

Oh! think of our favourite cottage,
  And think of our dear Lalla Rookh;

How we shared with the milkmaids their pottage,
And drank of the stream from the brook;
How fondly our loving lips faltered—
"What farther can grandeur bestow?"
My heart is the same—is yours altered?
My own Araminta, say "No!"

Remember the thrilling romances
We read on the bank in the glen;
Remember the suitors our fancies
Would picture for both of us then;
They wore the red cross on their shoulder,
They had vanquished and pardoned their foe—
Sweet friend, are you wiser or colder?
My own Araminta, say "No!"

You know, when Lord Rigmarole's carriage
Drove off with your cousin Justine,
You wept, dearest girl, at the marriage,
And whispered, "How base she has been!"
You said you were sure it would kill you
If ever your husband looked so;
And you will not apostatize, will you?
My own Araminta, say "No!"

When I heard I was going abroad, Love,
I thought I was going to die;
We walked arm-in-arm to the road, Love,

We looked arm-in-arm to the sky;
And I said, "When a foreign postilion
Has hurried me off to the Po,
Forget not Medora Trevilian;"—
My own Araminta, say "No!"

We parted! but sympathy's fetters
Reach far over valley and hill;
I muse o'er your exquisite letters,
And feel that your heart is mine still.
And he who would share it with me, Love,
The richest of treasures below,
If he's not what Orlando should be, Love,
My own Araminta, say "No!"

If he wears a top boot in his wooing,
If he comes to you riding a cob,
If he talks of his baking or brewing,
If he puts up his feet on the hob,
If he ever drinks port after dinner,
If his brow or his breeding is low,
If he calls himself "Thompson" or "Skinner,"
My dear Araminta, say "No!"

If he studies the news in the papers,
While you are preparing the tea,
If he talks of the damps or the vapours,
While moonlight lies soft on the sea,
If he's sleepy while you are capricious,

If he has not a musical "Oh!"
If he does not call Werther delicious,
My own Araminta, say "No!"

If he ever sets foot in the city,
Among the stockbrokers and Jews,
If he has not a heart full of pity,
If he don't stand six feet in his shoes,
If his lips are not redder than roses,
If his hands are not whiter than snow,
If he has not the model of noses,
My own Araminta, say "No!"

If he speaks of a tax or a duty,
If he does not look grand on his knees,
If he's blind to a landscape of beauty,
Hills, valleys, rocks, waters, and trees,
If he dotes not on desolate towers,
If he likes not to hear the blast blow,
If he knows not the language of flowers,
My own Araminta, say "No!"

He must walk like a god of old story,
Come down from the home of his rest;
He must smile like the sun in his glory,
On the buds he loves ever the best;
And, oh! from its ivory portal,
Like music his soft speech must flow!—
If he speak, smile, or walk like a mortal,
My own Araminta, say "No!"

Don't listen to tales of his bounty,
  Don't hear what they say of his birth,
Don't look at his seat in the county,
  Don't calculate what he is worth;
But give him a theme to write verse on,
  And see if he turns out his toe;—
If he's only an excellent person,
  My own Araminta, say "No!"

(1828.)

THE TALENTED MAN.

A LETTER FROM A LADY IN LONDON TO A LADY AT LAUSANNE.

Dear Alice! you'll laugh when you know it,—
  Last week, at the Duchess's ball,
I danced with the clever new poet,—
  You've heard of him,—Tully St. Paul.
Miss Jonquil was perfectly frantic;
  I wish you had seen Lady Anne!
It really was very romantic,
  He *is* such a talented man!

He came up from Brazen Nose College,
  Just caught, as they call it, this spring;
And his head, love, is stuffed full of knowledge
  Of every conceivable thing.

Of science and logic he chatters,
  As fine and as fast as he can;
Though I am no judge of such matters,
  I'm sure he's a talented man.

His stories and jests are delightful;—
  Not stories or jests, dear, for you;
The jests are exceedingly spiteful,
  The stories not always *quite* true.
Perhaps to be kind and veracious
  May do pretty well at Lausanne;
But it never would answer,—good gracious!
  Chez nous—in a talented man.

He sneers,—how my Alice would scold him!—
  At the bliss of a sigh or a tear;
He laughed—only think!—when I told him
  How we cried o'er Trevelyan last year;
I vow I was quite in a passion;
  I broke all the sticks of my fan;
But sentiment's quite out of fashion,
  It seems, in a talented man.

Lady Bab, who is terribly moral,
  Has told me that Tully is vain,
And apt—which is silly—to quarrel,
  And fond—which is sad—of champagne.
I listened, and doubted, dear Alice,
  For I saw, when my lady began,

It was only the Dowager's malice;—
  She *does* hate a talented man!

He's hideous, I own it. But fame, love,
  Is all that these eyes can adore;
He's lame,—but Lord Byron was lame, love,
  And dumpy,—but so is Tom Moore.
Then his voice,—*such* a voice! my sweet creature,
  It's like your Aunt Lucy's toucan:
But oh! what's a tone or a feature,
  When once one's a talented man?

My mother, you know, all the season,
  Has talked of Sir Geoffrey's estate;
And truly, to do the fool reason,
  He *has* been less horrid of late.
But to-day, when we drive in the carriage,
  I'll tell her to lay down her plan;—
If ever I venture on marriage,
  It must be a talented man!

P. S.—I have found, on reflection,
  One fault in my friend,—*entre nous;*
Without it, he'd just be perfection;—
  Poor fellow, he has not a *sou!*
And so, when he comes in September,
  To shoot with my uncle, Sir Dan,
I've promised mamma to remember
  He's *only* a talented man!

(1831.)

LETTERS FROM TEIGNMOUTH.

I.—OUR BALL.

"Comment! c'est lui? que je le regarde encore! C'est que vraiment il est bien changé; n'est ce pas, mon papa?"—*Les Premiers Amours.*

YOU'LL come to our ball;—since we parted
 I've thought of you more than I'll say;
Indeed, I was half broken-hearted
 For a week, when they took you away.
Fond fancy brought back to my slumbers
 Our walks on the Ness and the Den,
And echoed the musical numbers
 Which you used to sing to me then.
I know the romance, since it's over,
 'Twere idle, or worse, to recall;—
I know you're a terrible rover;
 But, Clarence, you'll come to our Ball!

It's only a year since, at College,
 You put on your cap and your gown;
But, Clarence, you're grown out of knowledge,
 And changed from the spur to the crown;
The voice that was best when it faltered,
 Is fuller and firmer in tone:

And the smile that should never have altered,—
  Dear Clarence,—it is not your own;
Your cravat was badly selected,
  Your coat don't become you at all;
And why is your hair so neglected?
  You must have it curled for our Ball.

I've often been out upon Haldon
  To look for a covey with Pup;
I've often been over to Shaldon,
  To see how your boat is laid up.
In spite of the terrors of Aunty,
  I've ridden the filly you broke;
And I've studied your sweet little Dante
  In the shade of your favourite oak:
When I sat in July to Sir Lawrence,
  I sat in your love of a shawl;
And I'll wear what you brought me from Flo-
  Perhaps, if you'll come to our Ball. [rence,

You'll find us all changed since you vanished;
  We've set up a National School;
And waltzing is utterly banished;
  And Ellen has married a fool;
The Major is going to travel;
  Miss Hyacinth threatens a rout;
The walk is laid down with fresh gravel;
  Papa is laid up with the gout:
And Jane has gone on with her easels,

And Anne has gone off with Sir Paul;
And Fanny is sick with the measles,
And I'll tell you the rest at the Ball.

You'll meet all your beauties;—the Lily,
And the Fairy of Willowbrook Farm,
And Lucy, who made me so silly
At Dawlish, by taking your arm;
Miss Manners, who always abused you,
For talking so much about Hock;
And her sister, who often amused you,
By raving of rebels and Rock;
And something which surely would answer,
An heiress quite fresh from Bengal;—
So, though you were seldom a dancer,
You'll dance, just for once, at our Ball.

But out on the world!—from the flowers
It shuts out the sunshine of truth;
It blights the green leaves in the bowers,
It makes an old age of our youth:
And the flow of our feeling, once in it,
Like a streamlet beginning to freeze,
Though it cannot turn ice in a minute,
Grows harder by sudden degrees.
Time treads o'er the graves of affection;
Sweet honey is turned into gall;
Perhaps you have no recollection
That ever you danced at our Ball.

You once could be pleased with our ballads—
  To-day you have critical ears;
You once could be charmed with our salads—
  Alas! you've been dining with Peers;
You trifled and flirted with many;
  You've forgotten the when and the how;
There was one you liked better than any—
  Perhaps you've forgotten her now.
But of those you remember most newly,
  Of those who delight or inthrall,
None love you a quarter so truly
  As some you will find at our Ball.

They tell me you've many who flatter,
  Because of your wit and your song;
They tell me (and what does it matter?)
  You like to be praised by the throng;
They tell me you're shadowed with laurel,
  They tell me you're loved by a Blue;
They tell me you're sadly immoral—
  Dear Clarence, that cannot be true!
But to me you are still what I found you
  Before you grew clever and tall;
And you'll think of the spell that once bound you:
  And you'll come, WON'T you come? to our Ball?

(1829.)

LETTERS FROM TEIGNMOUTH.

II.—PRIVATE THEATRICALS.

——Sweet, when Actors first appear,
The loud collision of applauding gloves!——*Moultrie.*

YOUR labours, my talented brother,
  Are happily over at last;
They tell me that, somehow or other,
  The bill is rejected,—or passed:
And now you'll be coming, I'm certain,
  As fast as your posters can crawl,
To help us to draw up our curtain,
  As usual, at Fustian Hall.

Arrangements are nearly completed;
  But still we've a lover or two,
Whom Lady Albina entreated
  We'd keep at all hazards for you:
Sir Arthur makes horrible faces,—
  Lord John is a trifle too tall,—
And yours are the safest embraces
  To faint in, at Fustian Hall.

Come, Clarence;—it's really enchanting
  To listen and look at the rout:
We're all of us puffing, and panting,

And raving, and running about;
Here Kitty and Adelaide bustle;
There Andrew and Anthony bawl;
Flutes murmur, chains rattle, robes rustle,
In chorus, at Fustian Hall.

By the by, there are two or three matters
We want you to bring us from town;
The Inca's white plume from the hatter's,
A nose and a hump for the Clown:
We want a few harps for our banquet,
We want a few masks for our ball;
And steal from your wise friend, Bosanquet,
His white wig, for Fustian Hall.

Hunca Munca must have a huge sabre,
Friar Tuck has forgotten his cowl;
And we're quite at a stand-still with Weber,
For want of a lizard and owl:
And then, for our funeral procession,
Pray get us a love of a pall;
Or how shall we make an impression
On feelings, at Fustian Hall?

And, Clarence, you'll really delight us,
If you'll do your endeavour to bring
From the Club a young person to write us
Our prologue, and that sort of thing:
Poor Crotchet, who did them supremely,

Is gone, for a judge, to Bengal;
I fear we shall miss him extremely,
This season, at Fustian Hall.

Come, Clarence;—your idol Albina
Will make a sensation, I feel;
We all think there never was seen a
Performer so like the O'Neill.
At rehearsals, her exquisite fancy
Has deeply affected us all;
For one tear that trickles at Drury,
There'll be twenty at Fustian Hall.

Dread objects are scattered before her,
On purpose to harrow her soul;
She stares, till a deep spell comes o'er her,
At a knife, or a cross, or a bowl.
The sword never seems to alarm her,
That hangs on a peg to the wall,
And she dotes on thy rusty old armour,
Lord Fustian, of Fustian Hall.

She stabbed a bright mirror this morning,—
Poor Kitty was quite out of breath,—
And trampled, in anger and scorning,
A bonnet and feathers to death.
But, hark!—I've a part in the Stranger,—
There's the Prompter's detestable call:
Come, Clarence,—our Romeo and Ranger,
We want you at Fustian Hall.

(1831.)

TALES OUT OF SCHOOL.

A DROPPED LETTER FROM A LADY.

YOUR godson, my sweet Lady Bridget,
  Was entered at Eton last May;
But really, I'm all in a fidget
  Till the dear boy is taken away;
For I feel an alarm which, I'm certain,
  A mother to you may confess,
When the newspaper draws up the curtain,
  The terrible Windsor Express.

You know I was half broken-hearted
  When the poor fellow whispered "Good-by!"
As soon as the carriage had started,
  I sat down in comfort to cry.
Sir Thomas looked on while I fainted,
  Deriding—the bear!—my distress;
But what were the hardships I painted,
  To the tales of the Windsor Express?

The planter in sultry Barbadoes
  Is a terrible tyrant, no doubt;
In Moscow, a Count carbonadoes
  His ignorant serfs with the knout;

Severely men smart for their errors,
  Who dine at a man-of-war's mess!
But Eton has crueller terrors
  Than these,—in the Windsor Express.

I fancied the Doctor at College
  Had dipped, now and then, into books;
But, bless me! I find that his knowledge
  Is just like my coachman's or cook's:
He's a dunce—I have heard it with sorrow;—
  'Twould puzzle him sadly, I guess,
To put into English to-morrow
  A page of the Windsor Express.

All preachers of course should be preaching
  That virtue's a very good thing;
All tutors of course should be teaching
  To fear God and honour the King;
But at Eton they've regular classes
  For folly, for vice, for excess;
They learn to be villains and asses,
  Nothing else—in the Windsor Express.

Mrs. Martha, who nursed little Willy,
  Believes that she nursed him in vain;
Old John, who takes care of the filly,
  Says "He'll ne'er come to mount her again!"
My Juliet runs up to her mother,
  And cries, with a mournful caress,

"Oh where have you sent my poor brother?
  Look, look at the Windsor Express!"

Ring, darling, and order the carriage;
  Whatever Sir Thomas may say,—
Who has been quite a fool since our marriage,—
  I'll take him directly away.
For of all their atrocious ill-treating,
  The end it is easy to guess;—
Some day they'll be killing and eating
  My boy—in the Windsor Express!

(Oct. 27, 1832.)

PALINODIA.

"Nec meus hic sermo est, sed quem præcepit."
Horace.

There was a time when I could feel
  All passion's hopes and fears,
And tell what tongues can ne'er reveal,
  By smiles, and sighs, and tears.
The days are gone! no more! no more,
  The cruel fates allow;
And though I'm hardly twenty-four,
  I'm not a lover now!

Lady, the mist is on my sight,
The chill is on my brow;
My day is night, my bloom is blight,
I'm not a lover now!

I never talk about the clouds,
I laugh at girls and boys;
I'm growing rather fond of crowds,
And very fond of noise—
I never wander forth alone
Upon the mountain's brow;
I weighed last winter sixteen stone—
I'm not a lover now!

I never wish to raise a veil,
I never raise a sigh,
I never tell a tender tale,
I never tell a lie;
I cannot kneel as once I did,
I've quite forgot my bow,
I never do as I am bid—
I'm not a lover now.

I make strange blunders every day,
If I would be gallant—
Take smiles for wrinkles, black for gray,
And nieces for their aunt;
I fly from folly, though it flows
From lips of loveliest glow;

I don't object to length of nose—
  I'm not a lover now!

I find my Ovid very dry,
  My Petrarch quite a pill,
Cut Fancy for Philosophy,
  Tom Moore for Mr. Mill.
And belles may read, and beaux may write—
  I care not who or how;
I burnt my album, Sunday night;
  I'm not a lover now!

I don't encourage idle dreams
  Of poison, or of ropes;
I cannot dine on airy schemes,
  I cannot sup on hopes!
New milk, I own, is very fine,
  Just foaming from the cow;
But yet, I want my pint of wine—
  I'm not a lover now!

When Laura sings young hearts away,
  I'm deafer than the deep;
When Leonora goes to play,
  I sometimes go to sleep;
When Mary draws her white gloves out,
  I never dance, I vow—
Too hot to kick one's heels about!—
  I'm not a lover now!

I'm busy now with State affairs,
  I prate of Pitt and Fox!
I ask the price of railroad shares,
  I watch the turns of stocks.
And this is life—no verdure blooms
  Upon the withered bough;
I save a fortune in perfumes—
  I'm not a lover now!

I may be yet what others are,
  A boudoir's babbling fool;
The flattered star of bench or bar,
  A party's chief or tool.
Come shower or sunshine—hope or fear,
  The palace or the plough,
My heart and lute are broken here—
  I'm not a lover now!
    Lady, the mist is on my sight,
      The chill is on my brow;
    My day is night, my bloom is blight,
      I'm not a lover now!

(1826.)

UTOPIA.

——"I can dream, sir,
If I eat well and sleep well."—*The Mad Lover.*

If I could scare the light away,
No sun should ever shine;
If I could bid the clouds obey,
Thick darkness should be mine:
Where'er my weary footsteps roam,
I hate whate'er I see;
And Fancy builds a fairer home
In slumber's hour for me.

I had a vision yesternight
Of a lovelier land than this,
Where heaven was clothed in warmth and light,
Where earth was full of bliss;
And every tree was rich with fruits,
And every field with flowers,
And every zephyr wakened lutes
In passion-haunted bowers.

I clambered up a lofty rock,
And did not find it steep;
I read through a page and a half of Locke,
And did not fall asleep;

I said whate'er I may but feel,
  I paid whate'er I owe;
And I danced one day an Irish reel,
  With the gout in every toe.

And I was more than six feet high,
  And fortunate and wise;
And I had a voice of melody,
  And beautiful black eyes;
My horses like the lightning went,
  My barrels carried true,
And I held my tongue at an argument,
  And winning cards at Loo.

I saw an old Italian priest
  Who spoke without disguise;
I dined with a judge who swore, like Best,
  All libels should be lies:
I bought for a penny a twopenny loaf,
  Of wheat and nothing more;
I danced with a female *philosophe*,
  Who was not quite a bore.

The kitchens there had richer roast,
  The sheep wore whiter wool;
I read a witty Morning Post,
  And an innocent John Bull;
The jailers had nothing at all to do,
  The hangman looked forlorn,

And the Peers had passed a vote or two
  For freedom of trade in corn.

There was a crop of wheat, which grew
  Where plough was never brought;
There was a noble Lord, who knew
  What he was never taught:
A scheme appeared in the Gazette
  For a lottery with no blanks;
And a Parliament had lately met,
  Without a single Bankes.

And there were kings who never went
  To cuffs for half-a-crown;
And lawyers who were eloquent
  Without a wig and gown;
And sportsmen who forbore to praise
  Their greyhounds and their guns;
And poets who deserved the bays,
  And did not dread the duns.

And boroughs were bought without a test,
  And no man feared the Pope;
And the Irish cabins were all possessed
  Of liberty and soap;
And the Chancellor, feeling very sick,
  Had just resigned the seals;
And a clever little Catholic
  Was hearing Scotch appeals.

I went one day to a Court of Law
  Where a fee had been refused;
And a Public School I really saw
  Where the rod was never used:
And the sugar still was very sweet,
  Though all the slaves were free;
And all the folk in Downing street
  Had learned the rule of three.

There love had never a fear or doubt;
  December breathed like June:
The Prima Donna ne'er was out
  Of temper—or of tune;
The streets were paved with mutton pies,
  Potatoes ate like pine;
Nothing looked black but woman's eyes;
  Nothing grew old but wine.

It was an idle dream; but thou,
  The worshipped one, wert there,
With thy dark clear eyes and beaming brow,
  White neck and floating hair;
And, oh! I had an honest heart,
  And a house of Portland stone;
And thou wert dear, as still thou art,
  And more than dear, my own!

Oh, bitterness!—the morning broke
  Alike for boor and bard;

And thou wert married when I woke,
  And all the rest was marred:
And toil and trouble, noise and steam,
  Came back with the coming ray;
And, if I thought the dead could dream,
  I'd hang myself to-day!

(1827.)

MARRIAGE CHIMES.

——— "Go together,
You precious winners all."—*Winter's Tale.*

Fair Lady, ere you put to sea,
  You and your mate together,
I meant to hail you lovingly,
  And wish you pleasant weather.
I took my fiddle from the shelf;
  But vain was all my labour;
For still I thought about myself,
  And not about my neighbour.

Safe from the perils of the war,
  Nor killed, nor hurt, nor missing—
Since many things in common are
  Between campaigns and kissing—

Ungrazed by glance, unbound by ring,
  Love's carte and tierce I've parried,
While half my friends are marrying,
  And half—good lack!—are married.

'Tis strange—but I have passed alive
  Where darts and deaths were plenty,
Until I find my twenty-five
  As lonely as my twenty:
And many lips have sadly sighed—
  Which were not made for sighing,
And many hearts have darkly died—
  Which never dreamed of dying.

Some victims fluttered like a fly,
  Some languished like a lily;
Some told their tale in poetry,
  And some in Piccadilly:
Some yielded to a Spanish hat,
  Some to a Turkish sandal;
Hosts suffered from an *entrechat*,
  And one or two from Handel.

Good Sterling said no dame should come
  To be the queen of his bourn,
But one who only prized her home,
  Her spinning-wheel, and Gisborne:
And Mrs. Sterling says odd things
  With most sublime effront'ry;

Gives lectures on elliptic springs,
  And follows hounds 'cross country.

Sir Roger had a Briton's pride
  In freedom, plough, and furrow;—
No fortune hath Sir Roger's bride,
  Except a rotten borough:
Gustavus longed for truth and crumbs,
  Contentment and a cottage;—
His Laura brings a pair of *plums*
  To boil the poor man's pottage.

My rural coz, who loves his peace,
  And swore at scientifics,
Is flirting with a lecturer's niece,
  Who construes hieroglyphics:
And Foppery's fool, who hated Blues
  Worse than he hated Holborn,
Is raving of a pensive Muse,
  Who does the verse for Colburn.

And Vyvyan, Humour's crazy child,—
  Whose worship, whim, or passion,
Was still for something strange and wild,
  Wit, wickedness, or fashion,—
Is happy with a little Love,
  A parson's pretty daughter,
As tender as a turtle-dove,—
  As dull as milk and water.

And Gerard hath his Northern Fay—
His nymph of mirth and haggis;
And Courtenay wins a damsel gay
Who figures at Colnaghi's;
And Davenant now has drawn a prize,—
I hope and trust, a Venus,
Because there are some sympathies—
As well as leagues—between us.

Thus north and south, and east and west,
The chimes of Hymen dingle;
But I shall wander on, unblest,
And singularly single;
Light-pursed, light-hearted, addle-brained,
And often captivated,
Yet, save on circuit—unretained,
And, save at chess—unmated.

Yet, oh!—if Nemesis with me
Should sport, as with my betters,
And put me on my awkward knee
To prate of flowers and fetters,—
I know not whose the eyes should be
To make this fortress tremble;
But yesternight I dreamed,—ah me!
Whose they should most resemble!

(November 20, 1827.)

SCHOOL AND SCHOOL-FELLOWS.

"Floreat Etona."

Twelve years ago I made a mock
  Of filthy trades and traffics;
I wondered what they meant by stock;
  I wrote delightful sapphics:
I knew the streets of Rome and Troy,
  I supped with fates and furies;
Twelve years ago I was a boy,
  A happy boy, at Drury's.

Twelve years ago!—how many a thought
  Of faded pains and pleasures
Those whispered syllables have brought
  From memory's hoarded treasures!
The fields, the farms, the bats, the books,
  The glories and disgraces,
The voices of dear friends, the looks
  Of old familiar faces!

Kind Mater smiles again to me,
  As bright as when we parted;
I seem again the frank, the free,
  Stout-limbed, and simple-hearted;

Pursuing every idle dream,
And shunning every warning;
With no hard work but Bovney Stream,
No chill except Long Morning:

Now stopping Harry Vernon's ball,
That rattled like a rocket;
Now hearing Wentworth's "Fourteen all,"
And striking for the pocket:
Now feasting on a cheese and flitch,
Now drinking from the pewter;
Now leaping over Chalvey ditch,
Now laughing at my tutor.

Where are my friends?—I am alone,
No playmate shares my beaker—
Some lie beneath the churchyard stone,
And some before the Speaker;
And some compose a tragedy,
And some compose a rondo;
And some draw sword for liberty,
And some draw pleas for John Doe.

Tom Mill was used to blacken eyes,
Without the fear of sessions;
Charles Medler loathed false quantities,
As much as false professions.
Now Mill keeps order in the land,
A magistrate pedantic;

And Medler's feet repose, unscanned,
  Beneath the wide Atlantic.

Wild Nick, whose oaths made such a din,
  Does Dr. Martext's duty;
And Mullion, with that monstrous chin,
  Is married to a beauty;
And Darrel studies, week by week,
  His Mant, and not his Manton;
And Ball, who was but poor at Greek,
  Is very rich at Canton.

And I am eight-and-twenty now—
  The world's cold chains have bound me;
And darker shades are on my brow,
  And sadder scenes around me:
In Parliament I fill my seat,
  With many other noodles;
And lay my head in Jermyn-street,
  And sip my hock at Boodle's.

But often, when the cares of life
  Have set my temples aching,
When visions haunt me of a wife,
  When duns await my waking,
When Lady Jane is in a pet,
  Or Hoby in a hurry,
When Captain Hazard wins a bet,
  Or Beaulieu spoils a curry:

For hours and hours I think and talk
  Of each remembered hobby;
I long to lounge in Poet's Walk—
  To shiver in the lobby;
I wish that I could run away
  From house, and court, and levee,
Where bearded men appear to-day,
  Just Eton boys, grown heavy;

That I could bask in childhood's sun,
  And dance o'er childhood's roses;
And find huge wealth in one pound one,
  Vast wit in broken noses;
And play Sir Giles at Datchet Lane,
  And call the milkmaids houris;
That I could be a boy again—
  A happy boy at Drury's!

(1829.)

PROLOGUE

FOR AN AMATEUR PERFORMANCE OF "THE HONEYMOON."

"We want"—the Duchess said to me to-day,—
"We want, fair sir, a prologue for our play.
A charming play to show a charming robe in,
'The Honeymoon' "—"By Phœbus!"—"No: by Tobin."
"A prologue!"—I made answer—"if you need one,
In every street and square your Grace may read one."

"Cruel papa! don't talk about Sir Harry!"—
So Araminta lisped;—"I'll never marry;
I loathe all men; such unromantic creatures!
The coarsest tastes, and, ah! the coarsest features!
Betty!—the salts!—I'm sick with mere vexation,
To hear them called the Lords of the Creation:
They swear fierce oaths, they seldom say their prayers;
And then, they shed no tears,—unfeeling bears!

I, and the friend I share my sorrows with,
Medora Gertrude Wilhelmina Smith,
Will weep together through the world's disasters,
In some green vale, unplagued by Lords and Masters,
And hand in hand repose at last in death,
As chaste and cold as Queen Elizabeth."
She spoke in May, and people found in June,
This was *her* Prologue to the Honeymoon!

"Frederic is poor, I own it," Fanny sighs,
"But then he loves me, and has deep blue eyes.
Since I was nine years old, and he eleven,
We've loved each other,—'Love is light from Heaven!'
And penury with love, I will not doubt it,
Is better far than palaces without it.
We'll have a quiet curacy in Kent;
We'll keep a cow; and we'll be *so* content!
Forgetting that my father drove fine horses,
And that my mother dined upon three courses,
There I shall sit, perusing Frederic's verses,
Dancing in spring, in winter knitting purses;
Mending the children's pinafores and frills,
Wreathing sweet flowers, and paying butcher's bills."
Alas, poor Fanny! she will find too soon
Her Prologue's better than her Honeymoon.

But, lo! where Laura, with a frenzied air,
Seeks her kind cousin in her pony chair,
And in a mournful voice, by thick sobs broken,
Cries "Yes, dear Anne! the favours are bespoken;
I *am* to have him;—so my friends decided;
The stars knew quite as much of it as I did!
You know him, love;—he is so like a mummy;—
I wonder whether diamonds will become me!
He talks of nothing but the price of stocks;
However, I'm to have my opera box.
That pert thing, Ellen, thought she could secure him,—
I wish she had, I'm sure I can't endure him!
The cakes are ordered;—how my lips will falter
When I stand fainting at the marriage altar!
But I'm to have him! Oh, the vile baboon!"
Strange Prologue this for Laura's Honeymoon!

Enough of Prologues; surely I should say
One word, before I go, about the play.
Instead of hurrying madly after marriage
To some lord's villa in a travelling carriage,
Instead of seeking earth's remotest ends
To hide their blushes and avoid their friends,
Instead of haunting lonely lanes and brooks
With no companions but the doves and rooks,—

Our Duke and Duchess open wide their Hall,
And bid you warmly welcome, one and all,
Who come with hearts of kindness, eyes of light,
To see, and share, *their* Honeymoon to-night.

(January 19, 1830.)

POEMS WRITTEN IN EARLY YOUTH.

ON PITY.

Sweet is it to the warrior's ear
  To mark the clamorous battle-cry,
But sweeter far the crystal tear
  That falls from Pity's moistened eye;
And savage is the cruel beast
  That prowls round Gondar's lofty tower,
But harder far that human breast
  That ne'er has felt soft Pity's power.

But see, with ostentatious sneer
  Will Laura precious gifts bestow;
Emilia often sheds the tear,
  But affectation bids it flow.
These do not own compassion's reign;
  True pity acts not such a part;
It flies the rich, it flies the vain,—
  It dwells in kind Sophia's heart.

Whene'er the poor, worn out with woe,
  Oppressed with trouble, years, and grief,
From breasts which feel compassion's glow
  Solicit mild the kind relief,—
Then Laura opes her ready hand,
  The tear bedews Emilia's eye;

Sophia quits the selfish band
  To soothe the pangs of Poverty.

Gold can but present help afford;
  Emilia's tear is wiped away;
Sophia feels her just reward,
  A bliss which never will decay.
This, the reward of virtue, this
  Th' unfeeling heart will never know:
It is the only earthly bliss
  Which is not mixed with earthly woe.

(1815.)

ON THE DEPARTURE OF AN OLD HOUSEKEEPER.

'Tis past; and since she is forever fled,
With all her by-gone blunders on her head,
Let not the laugh, the sneer, pursue her still,
Nor mark her failings, where she meant no ill.
Cease now her foibles, Ridicule, to tell;
Let Gratitude declare—she loved us well.

Can we forget, now when for aye we part,
Her charity, the goodness of her heart,

Her wish to please, her readiness to lend
(Although unasked) assistance to a friend?
Can we forget all these? and yet retain
The few—the puny errors of her brain?
You who are blind to what her heart could do,
Be just at least, dismiss her failings too:
Grant—while an inmate, her mistakes could tease,
Her look amuse us, or her faults displease,—
Yet now—her fancies and her follies past—
Her failings vanish, while her love will last.
Still, when she calls to mind her happiest days,
She'll load her former friends with well-meant praise;
Still will regret that, forced at length to roam,
She leaves the spot she called so long her home.

Let us our ridicule, our mocking, end;
Quit the companion, yet retain the friend;
Forgive her faults, for there no malice lowers;
Forget those faults, for she was blind to ours.

(1816.)

VALENTINES.

I.—IMITATION OF METASTASIO'S "PARTENZA."

SISTER, far from thee I'm gone;
And often, silent and alone,
Sudden starts a willing tear
Which would not fall if thou wert here;
    But thou, my Susan, who can tell
    If thy least thought on me shall dwell?

How quick our meeting days have passed!
But human pleasures will not last;
And Learning's all-consuming power
Hastened on our parting hour.
    But thou, my Susan, who can tell
    If thy least thought on me shall dwell?

But quickly still, from day to day,
Flies the hasty time away;
Fraught with hope and sportive glee,
I'll soon revisit home and thee;
    Whilst thou, my Susan, who can tell
    If thy least thought on me shall dwell?

But stay, I wrong thee, gentle dove,
I know I wrong thy tender love;
Oft thine eye will shed a tear,
Which would not fall if I were near;
Yes, yes, my Susan, I can tell,
Oft thy thoughts on me will dwell.

(February 14, 1816.)

II.—A MADRIGAL.

When weeping friends are parting,
Oh, then their hearts are smarting!
But when they're just returning,
Oh, then their hearts are burning!
They're merry all,
Nor once recall
The tear they shed at parting.

(February 14, 1817.)

III.—THE DOVE.

Tell me, little darling Dove,
Whence and whither dost thou rove?

I am in haste; a brother tied
This doggerel greeting to my side;
May every good my sister bless,—
Life, virtue, health, and happiness;
Not vulgar mirth, but modest sense;
Not mines of gold, but competence;
With these her bark may peaceful glide,
Uninjured, down life's swelling tide.
May soft Content's all-healing power
Stand ready for each suffering hour,
Enhance the good the Fates bestow,
And mitigate the pangs of woe.
Each year may an adoring crew
New Valentines around her strew;
Be every page, be every line,
As ardent, as sincere, as mine!

(February 14, 1817.)

IV.—THE DEITIES.

Each god has left his heavenly seat,
  Olympus, for a while;
And animates a mortal shape
  In Britain's favoured isle;
Ye Deities, no thin disguise
Conceals ye from a poet's eyes!

Jove thunders as Britannia's King,
  And Bacchus is his son;
And Byron strikes Apollo's lyre;
  And Mars is Wellington.
Like Neptune, Exmouth rules the sea,—
But lovely Venus smiles in thee.

Yet not alone does Venus smile;
  For there are joined in thee
The Muses' verse, Minerva's sense,
  And Juno's majesty:
The Graces o'er thy figure rove,
And every feature beams with Love.

(1817.)

A FABLE.

TO HIS ELDEST SISTER ON HER BIRTHDAY.

Virtue (a nymph you well must know)
Met gently warbling Erato;
And after bows, and "how d'ye do's,"
She thus addressed the smiling Muse:
"How is it,—tell me, Erato,—
That you and I such strangers grow?
If at your Mount my foot I set,
Flat 'Not at home' is all I get:
When first you called a meeting there,
And Phœbus deigned to take the chair,
The sire of men, of gods the king,
Your patron, Jove,—he bade you sing
Not those who in false glory shine,
But those who bow to Virtue's shrine;
And scorn you Jove? For now I deem
That Virtue is your rarest theme!
Calliopé, when war she sings,
Forgets the truth to flatter kings;
Euterpe thinks me low and mean,
Thalia drives me from her scene,
Melpomene like Folly rants,
Dishonest Clio scrawls romance;

E'en your own soft, enticing measure
Has left poor me, and flows for Pleasure."

"Cease your upbraidings!" cries the Muse:
"An ear at least you can't refuse:
I'll answer you for all the Nine;
The few who bow at Virtue's shrine
Are better pleased with artless praise
Than all the force of studied lays.
The page of silver-flowing rhyme
May hide a fault, or gild a crime;
But you, and those who choose your part,
Require the language of the heart;
And such will smile, and read with pleasure,
If 'tis sincere, a doggerel measure;
Though only on the page they view
Congratulation—and Adieu!"

(1817.)

LINES ON LEAVING OTTERTON.

Sweet spot, whose real joy excels
What Fancy's pencil ever drew,
Where Innocence with Pleasure dwells,
And Peace with Poverty—adieu!
If perfect bliss resides on earth,
Here lies the spot that gives it birth.

And you, whose presence throws a gleam
Of pleasure o'er the poor man's lot,
Who well to Fancy's eye might seem
The Genii of the peaceful spot,—
Fond Memory oft will bring to view
The welcome that we found with you.

It is not yours in hall or bower
The semblance of a smile to wear;
But yours it is, in sorrow's hour,
To stop the sufferer's falling tear:
Nor yours the fleeting, vain reward
That earthly power and pomp award.

From pomp and power men are riven
At every change of Fortune's will;

One purer bliss to you is given,
A heart that acts not, thinks not, ill.
The tyrant well for such a gem
Might quit his blood-bought diadem.

But we must part at length; 'tis sad
Upon such scenes as these to dwell,
Since scenes like these can only add
New sorrow to our long farewell:
Pure was our happiness—no more!
We part; that happiness is o'er.

We go; but we shall not forget
Those symptoms of a friendly heart,
The smile you wore because we met,
The tear you shed because we part;
And Hope already paints how sweet
The hour when we again shall meet.

(1817.)

FORGET ME NOT.

When thy sad master's far away,
Go, happier far than he,—
Go, little flower, with her to stay
With whom he may not be;
There bid her mourn his wayward lot,
And whisper still, "Forget me not!"

Sweet as the gale of fate, that blew
To waft me to a spot like this,—
Frail as the hours, that quickly flew
To tear me from the transient bliss,—
Thy humble blossoms long shall prove
An emblem fit for parted love.

(1817.)

WOMAN.

A FRAGMENT.

WOMAN! thou loveliest gift that here below
Man can receive, or Providence bestow!
To thee the earliest offerings belong
Of opening eloquence, or youthful song;
Lovely partaker of our dearest joys!
Thyself a gift whose pleasure never cloys,—
Whose wished-for presence gently can appease
The wounds of penury, or slow disease,—
Whose loss is such, as through life's tedious way
No rank can compensate, no wealth repay;
Thy figure beams a ray of heavenly light
To cheer the darkness of our earthly night:
Hail, fair Enslaver! at thy changing glance
Boldness recedes, and timid hearts advance,
Monarchs forget their sceptre and their sway,
And sages melt in tenderness away.

(1818.)

MUNITO.

FROM A POEM ON DOGS.

Though great Spadille, or that famed Prince of
 Loo,
All-conquering Pam, turn backward from his
 view,—
Swift in the noble chase, Munito tracks
The Royal guests amid Plebeian packs;
And though the cards in mixed confusion lie,
And mock the vigour of a human eye,
Munito still, with more than human art,
Knows Kings from Knaves, the Diamond from
 the Heart:
Happy were men, if thus in graver things
Our Knaves were always parted from our Kings;
Happy the maid, who in Love's maze can part
The miser's Diamond from the lover's Heart!

(1818.)

LINES

WRITTEN IN THE FIRST LEAF OF VOLTAIRE'S "HISTOIRE DE CHARLES XII."

Thou little Book, thy leaves unfold
A tale of wonder and of glory,
And warring kings and barons bold
Adorn the pages of thy story.

Thy vein is noble; meet and fit
To catch and charm a youthful eye;
Thou teem'st with wonder and with wit;
And yet I look on thee, and sigh:

Thy tales are sweet, but they renew
Visions how sad! yet, ah, how dear!
Vain fancies mock my wandering view,
And recollection wakes a tear.

Thou bidd'st me think upon the hours
When giddy Tizy round me ran;
When glad I left Etona's bowers,
To laugh with laughing Mary Anne:

When Susan's voice of tenderness
My darkest sorrows could beguile;

When study wore its fairest dress,
  Adorned by good Eliza's smile.

Alas! too soon before mine eye
  Was spread the page of ancient lore;
Too soon that meeting fleeted by,
  Too soon those dreams of bliss were o'er.

I look on thee, and think again
  Upon those halcyon days of gladness,
While Memory mingles joy and pain,
  A mournful bliss, a pleasing sadness.

Ye friends with whom I may not be,
  Ye forms that I have loved and left,
What pleasure now shall beam on me,
  Of home and of your smiles bereft?

My lot and yours are parted now;
  And, oh! I should not thus repine,
If Fortune would on you bestow
  The happiness—which is not mine.

Long weeks must pass, ere I may greet
  The glad return of former bliss,—
Ere I may fly again to meet
  A cousin's smile, a sister's kiss.

(Eton, 1820.)

TO FLORENCE.

Long years have passed with silent pace,
  Florence, since thou and I have met;
Yet—when that meeting I retrace,
  My cheek is pale, my eye is wet;
For I was doomed from thence to rove,
  O'er distant tracts of earth and sea,
Unaided, Florence!—save by love;
  And unremembered—save by thee!
We met! and hope beguiled our fears,
  Hope, ever bright and ever vain;
We parted thence in silent tears,
  Never to meet—in life—again.
The myrtle that I gaze upon,
  Sad token by thy love devised,
Is all the record left of one
  So long bewailed—so dearly prized.
You gave it in an hour of grief,
  When gifts of love are doubly dear;
You gave it—and one tender leaf
  Glistened the while with Beauty's tear.
A tear—oh, lovelier far to me,
  Shed for me in my saddest hour,
Than bright and flattering smiles could be,
  In courtly hall or summer bower.

You strove my anguish to beguile,
  With distant hopes of future weal;
You strove!—alas! you could not smile,
  Nor speak the hope you did not feel.
I bore the gift Affection gave,
  O'er desert sand and thorny brake,
O'er rugged rock and stormy wave,
  I loved it for the giver's sake;
And often in my happiest day,
  In scenes of bliss and hours of pride,
When all around was glad and gay,
  I looked upon the gift—and sighed:
And when on ocean, or on clift,
  Forth strode the Spirit of the Storm,
I gazed upon thy fading gift,
  I thought upon thy fading form;
Forgot the lightning's vivid dart,
  Forgot the rage of sky and sea,
Forgot the doom that bade us part—
  And only lived to love and thee.
Florence! thy myrtle blooms! but thou,
  Beneath thy cold and lowly stone,
Forgetful of our mutual vow,
  And of a heart—still all thine own,
Art laid in that unconscious sleep,
  Which he that wails thee soon must know,
Where none may smile and none may weep,
  None dream of bliss, nor wake to woe.
If e'er, as Fancy oft will feign,

To that dear spot which gave thee birth
Thy fleeting shade returns again,
To look on him thou lov'dst on earth,
It may a moment's joy impart,
To know that this, thy favourite tree,
Is to my desolated heart
Almost as dear as thou couldst be.
My Florence!—soon—the thought is sweet!
The turf that wraps thee I shall press;
Again, my Florence! we shall meet,
In bliss—or in forgetfulness.
With thee in Death's oblivion laid,
I will not have the cypress gloom
To throw its sickly, sullen shade
Over the stillness of my tomb:
And there the 'scutcheon shall not shine,
And there the banner shall not wave;
The treasures of the glittering mine
Would ill become a lover's grave:
But when from this abode of strife
My liberated shade shall roam,
Thy myrtle, that has cheered my life,
Shall decorate my narrow home:
And it shall bloom in beauty there,
Like Florence in her early day;
Or, nipped by cold December's air,
Wither—like Hope and thee—away.

(1820.)

MARIUS AMIDST THE RUINS OF CARTHAGE.

Carthage! I love thee! thou hast run,
  As I, a warlike race;
And now thy Glory's radiant sun
  Hath veiled in clouds his face;
Thy days of pride—as mine—depart;
Thy gods desert thee, and thou art
  A thing as nobly base
As he whose sullen footstep falls
To-night around thy crumbling walls.

And Rome hath heaped her woes and pains
  Alike on me and thee;
And *thou* dost sit in servile chains,—
  But mine they shall not be!
Though fiercely o'er this aged head
The wrath of angry Jove is shed,
  Marius shall still be free,
Free,—in the pride that scorns his foe,
And bares the head to meet the blow.

I wear not yet thy slavery's vest,
  As desolate I roam;

And though the sword were at my breast,
  The torches in my home,
Still—still, for orison and vow,
I'd fling them back my curse—as now;
  I scorn, I hate thee—Rome!
My voice is weak to word and threat—
My arm is strong to battle yet!

(1821.)

EDWARD MORTON.

"November 26.—Heard of the death of poor Morton. If ever man died of love, it was Edward Morton. Since his death, a small collection of poems, written by him at different periods of his life, has been put into my hands; which I shall insert from time to time, with the signature 'E. M.'"—*The Etonian*, vol. i. pp. 313, 374.

I.

There was a voice—a foolish voice—
  In my heart's summer echoing through me;
It bade me hope, it bade rejoice,
  And still its sounds were precious to me;
But thou hast plighted that deep vow,
And it were sin to love thee now!

I will not love thee! I am taught
  To shun the dream on which I doted,
And tear my soul from every thought
  On which its dearest vision floated;
And I have prayed to look on thee
As coldly as thou dost on me.

Alas! the love indeed is gone,
  But still I feel its melancholy;
And the deep struggle, long and lone,
  That stifled all my youthful folly,
Took but away the guilt of sin,
And left me all its pain within.

Adieu! if thou hadst seen the heart—
  The silly heart thou wert beguiling,
Thou wouldst not have inflamed the smart
  With all thy bright, unconscious smiling;
Thou wouldst not so have fanned the blaze
That grew beneath those quiet rays!

Nay, it was well!—for smiles like this
  Delayed at least my bosom's fever!
Nay, it was well, since hope and bliss
  Were fleeting quickly, and forever,
To snatch them as they passed away,
And meet the anguish all to-day!

II.

I do not weep; the grief I feel
Is not the grief that dims the eye;
No accents speak, no tears reveal
The inward pain that cannot die.

Mary! thou know'st not—none can know
The silent woe that still must live;
I would not change that silent woe
For all the joy the world can give.

Yet, by thine hair so lightly flowing,
And by thy smiling lips, I vow,
And by thy cheek so brightly glowing,
And by the meekness of thy brow,

And by those eyes, whose tranquil beam
So joyfully is wont to shine,
As if thy bosom could not dream
Of half the woe that preys on mine,

I do not murmur that another
Hath gained the love I could not wake;
I look on him as on a brother,
And do not hate him—for thy sake.

And, Mary, when I gaze on thee,
I think not on my own distress;
Serene—in thy serenity,
And happy—in thine happiness.

III.

A FLOWER, in Nature's fairest dress,
  Bloomed on its parent tree;
Brightly it blushed in loveliness—
  That blush was not for me!
Oh! not for me, right well I knew;
And yet I watched it where it grew,
  Fondly and fearfully;
And often from my heart I prayed
That gentle Flower might never fade.

I could have borne to see it bloom
  By other hands caressed,
Giving its blossoms and perfume
  To deck another's breast;
And when that Flower, in future days,
Had met my melancholy gaze,
  Still living and still blest,
I should have spoke a calmer tone,
And made its happiness my own.

But thus to find it hurled away
  By him to whom it clung,
To watch it withering day by day,
  So beautiful and young!
To see it dying, yet repress
The agony of tenderness
  That lingers on the tongue!—

Alas! and doth it come to this,
Mary, thy cherished dream of bliss!

Gone is the colour from thy cheek,
  The lustre from thine eye;
Thy brow is cold, thy step is weak,
  Thy beauty passeth by!
In ignorance supremely blest,
Thy child is slumbering on thy breast,
  And feels not "she will die!"
Alas! alas!—I know not how
I speak of this so coldly now!

I love to muse on thee by night!
  And, while my bosom aches,
There is a something of delight
  In thinking why it breaks;
Therefore doth Reason come in vain;—
I dote on this consuming pain;
  Cling to the wounds it makes;
Talk—dream of it, and find relief
E'en in the bitterness of grief.

Where are ye now, ye coldly wise,
  Who bid the passions sleep,
Who scorn the mourner when he sighs,
  And call it crime to weep?
Yours is the lifelessness of life!—
I will not change this inward strife

For all your precepts deep,
Nor lose, in my departing years,
The pain--the bliss—the throb of tears!

IV.

I SAW thee wedded—thou didst go
Within the sacred aisle,
Thy young cheek in a blushing glow
Betwixt a tear and smile.
Thy heart was glad in maiden glee,
But he it loved so fervently
Was faithless all the while;
I hate him for the vow he spoke—
I hate him for the vow he broke.

I hid the love that could not die,
Its doubts, and hopes, and fears,
And buried all my misery
In secrecy and tears;
And days passed on, and thou didst prove
The pang of unrequited love
E'en in thine early years;
And thou didst die—so fair and good—
In silence, and in solitude!

While thou wert living, I did hide
Affection's secret pains:
I'd not have shocked thy modest pride
For all the world contains;

But thou hast perished, and the fire
That, often checked, could ne'er expire,
  Again unhidden reigns:
It is no crime to speak my vow,
For, ah! thou canst not hear it now.

Thou sleepest 'neath thy lowly stone
  That dark and dreamless sleep;
And he, thy loved and chosen one—
  Why goes he not to weep?
He does not kneel where I have knelt;
He cannot feel what I have felt,
  The anguish still and deep,
The painful thoughts of what has been,
The canker-worm that is not seen!

But I—as o'er the dark blue wave
  Unconsciously I ride,
My thoughts are hovering o'er thy grave,
  My soul is by thy side.
There is one voice that wails thee yet,
One heart that cannot e'er forget
  The visions that have died;
And aye thy form is buried there—
A doubt—an anguish—a despair!

(1820, 1821.)

A CHILD'S GRAVE.

O'ER yon Churchyard the storm may lower;
  But, heedless of the wintry air,
  One little bud shall linger there,
A still and trembling flower.

Unscathed by long revolving years,
  Its tender leaves shall flourish yet,
  And sparkle in the moonlight, wet
With the pale dew of tears.

And where thine humble ashes lie,
  Instead of 'scutcheon or of stone,
  It rises o'er thee, lonely one,
Child of obscurity!

Mild was thy voice as Zephyr's breath,
  Thy cheek with flowing locks was shaded!
  But the voice hath died, the cheek hath faded
In the cold breeze of death!

Brightly thine eye was smiling, Sweet!
  But now Decay hath stilled its glancing;
  Warmly thy little heart was dancing,
But it hath ceased to beat!

A few short months—and thou wert here!
  Hope sat upon thy youthful brow;
  And what is thy memorial now?
A flower—and a Tear.

A LETTER FROM ETON.

My dearest Cynthia,—
If you knew
Half of the toil P. C. goes through,
You'd never dip your spiteful pen
In Anger's bitter ink again,
Because the hapless author woos
No correspondent—save the Muse.

Was ever such a wretched elf?
I ha'n't a minute to myself!
My own and other people's cares
Are dinned incessant in my ears!
I can't get rid of Mr. Vapour,
With all his silly "midnight taper,"
Nor Mr. Musgrave's learned paper,
"Diseases of the Hoof;"
E'en now, as thus I sit me down,
Scared by your thunder and your frown,
Two Fiends are hid aloof;
Two Fiends in dark Cocytus dipped;
A Blockhead with a manuscript,
A Devil with a proof!
Alas! alas! I seem to find
Some torment for my wearied mind

In every thing I see!
My duck is old—my mutton tough,—
To some they may be good enough,
They smell of "Press" to me;
And when I stoop my lips to drink,
I often shudder as I think
I taste the taste of Printer's ink
In chocolate and tea!
And what with friends, and foes, and hits
Sent slyly out by little wits,
A fulminating breed;
And what with Critics, Queries, Quarrels,
Fame and fair faces, loves and laurels,
Sermons and sonnets, good and bad,
I'm getting—not a little mad—
But very mad indeed!

But you, who in your home of ease
Are far from sorrows such as these,
Maid of the archly smiling brow,
What folly are you following now?
With you, amid the mazy dance,
That came to us from clever France,
Does he, that bright and brilliant star,
The future Tully of the Bar,
Its present Vestris, glide?
Or does he quibble, stride, look big,
Assume the face of legal prig,
And charm you with his embryo wig,

In all its powdered pride?
Is he the Coryphæus still
Of winding Waltz, and gay Quadrille?
And is he talking fooleries
Of Ladies' love, and looks, and eyes,
And flirting with your fan?
Or does he prate of whens and whys,
Cross-questions, queries, and replies,
Cro. Car.—Cro. Jac.—and *Cro. Eliz.*,
To puzzle all he can?
Is he the favourite of to-day,
Or do you smile with kinder ray
On him, the grave Divine;
Whose periods sure were formed alike
In pulpit to amaze and strike,
In drawing-room to shine?
Alas! alas! methinks I see,
Amid those walks of revelry,
A dignitary's fall;
For, lingering long in fashion's scene,
He'll die a dancer, not a dean,
And find it hard to choose between
Preferment—and a ball!

I do not bid thee weep, my dear,
I would not see a single tear
In eyes so bright as those;
Nor dim the ray that love hath lit,
Nor check the stream of mirth and wit

That sparkles as it flows.
Be still the Fairy of the dance,
And keep that light and merry glance,
Yet do not, in your pride of place,
Forget your parted lover's face,
A poor one though it be!
Among the thousands that adore,
Believe not one can love you more;
And when, retired from ball and rout,
You've nothing else to think about,—
Why, waste a thought on me!

(June 25, 1821.)

ON THE DEATH OF A SCHOOLFELLOW.

TRANSLATED FROM SOME LATIN VERSES BY THE REV. E. C. HAWTREY.

Snatched from us in thy sinless years,
To thee we bid the lament flow,
And swell with unavailing tears
A brother's and a parent's woe.

'Tis sweet, poor Boy! and yet 'tis pain,
  Though life and hope are fled, e'en now
To cling with rapture, long and vain,
  Upon thy moistened cheek and brow;

Until we fancy that a gleam
  Again hath lit that glazing eye,
And call upon thy lips, and dream
  We hear those lifeless lips reply.

Yet, while the words are on my tongue,
  Corruption awes me! and aside
I shrink from that to which I clung,
  And feel what love would wish to hide.

And, while thy cold remains we lay
  To sleep beneath their colder stone,
I turn me from the frame's decay,
  To muse on that which knoweth none.

Unhurt, undying, undecayed,
  Thy soul exists beyond the tomb!
And, while I wander down the glade,
  Whose beauties now are wrapt in gloom,

Thy spirit comes at evening's hour,
  And thus it says, or seems to say:
"Lament not, though the cherished flower
  Hath bloomed and faded in a day;

"And let not them that gave me birth,
  And let not her that closed my eyes,
Weep o'er me in my bed of earth,
  Or sorrow at my obsequies!

"The rays of Heaven around me shine,—
  Why should they pine in earthly cares?
Eternity of bliss is mine,—
  Why should a moment's pang be theirs?"

(1821.)

SONNET.

If when with thee I feel and speak
What not with others I have felt and spoken,
It is not for the beauty of thy cheek,
Nor for thy forehead fair,
Nor for the dark locks quietly sleeping there,
Nor for thy words of kindness, Friendship's
    token;
But rather, that I trace
Passion and purity in that meaning face;
And that thy brow is stamped with feeling
Such as mocks the tongue's revealing,
And that I see in thy young soul
A breathing part of that celestial Whole,
And that thou art a Poet, and the son
Of an Immortal one!

(Cambridge, *December*, 1821.)

PRIZE POEMS, TRANSLATIONS,

AND

EPIGRAMS.

AUSTRALASIA.*

THE sun is high in heaven; a favouring breeze
Fills the white sail, and sweeps the rippling
seas,
And the tall vessel walks her destined way,
And rocks and glitters in the curling spray.
Among the shrouds, all happiness and hope,
The busy seaman coils the rattling rope,
And tells his jest, and carols out his song,
And laughs his laughter, vehement and long;
Or pauses on the deck, to dream awhile
Of his babes' prattle, and their mother's smile,
And nods the head, and waves the welcome hand,
To those who weep upon the lessening strand.

His is the roving step and humour dry,
His the light laugh, and his the jocund eye;
And his the feeling, which, in guilt or grief,
Makes the sin venial, and the sorrow brief.
But there are hearts, that merry deck below,
Of darker error, and of deeper woe,—
Children of wrath and wretchedness, who grieve
Not for the country, but the crimes they leave,—

* This poem obtained the Chancellor's Medal at the Cambridge Commencement, July, 1823.

Who, while for them, on many a sleepless bed,
The prayer is murmured, and the tear is shed,
In exile and in misery, lock within
Their dread despair, their unrepented sin,—
And in their madness dare to gaze on heaven,
Sullen and cold, unawed and unforgiven!

There the gaunt robber, stern in sin and shame,
Shows his dull features and his iron frame;
And tenderer pilferers creep in silence by,
With quivering lip, flushed brow, and vacant eye.
And some there are who, in their close of day,
With dropping jaw, weak step, and temples gray,
Go tottering forth to find, across the wave,
A short sad sojourn, and a foreign grave;
And some who look their long and last adieu
To the white cliffs that vanish from the view,
While youth still blooms, and vigour nerves the arm,
The blood flows freely, and the pulse beats warm.
The hapless female stands in silence there,
So weak, so wan, and yet so sadly fair,
That those who gaze—a rude, untutored tribe—
Check the coarse question, and the wounding gibe,
And look, and long to strike the fetter off,
And stay to pity, though they came to scoff.
Then o'er her cheek there runs a burning blush,
And the hot tears of shame begin to rush

Forth from their swelling orbs;—she turns away,
And her white fingers o'er her eyelids stray,
And still the tears through those white fingers
glide,
Which strive to check them, or at least to hide!

And there the stripling, led to plunder's school
Ere passion slept, or reason learned to rule,
Clasps his young hands, and beats his throbbing
brain,
And looks with marvel on his galling chain.
Oh! you may guess, from that unconscious gaze,
His soul hath dreamed of those far fading days,
When, rudely nurtured on the mountain's brow,
He tended day by day his father's plough;
Blest in his day of toil, his night of ease,
His life of purity, his soul of peace.
Oh, yes! to-day his soul hath backward been
To many a tender face, and beauteous scene;
The verdant valley and the dark-brown hill,
The small fair garden, and its tinkling rill,
His grandame's tale, believed at twilight hour,
His sister singing in her myrtle bower,
And she, the maid, of every hope bereft,
So fondly loved, alas! so falsely left;
The winding path, the dwelling in the grove,
The look of welcome, and the kiss of love—
These are his dreams;—but these are dreams of
bliss!
Why do they blend with such a lot as his?

And is there naught for him but grief and gloom,
A lone existence, and an early tomb?
Is there no hope of comfort and of rest
To the seared conscience, and the troubled breast?
Oh, say not so! In some far distant clime,
Where lives no witness of his early crime,
Benignant Penitence may haply muse
On purer pleasures, and on brighter views,
And slumbering Virtue wake at last to claim
Another being and a fairer fame.

Beautiful land! within whose quiet shore
Lost spirits may forget the stain they bore:
Beautiful land! with all thy blended shades
Of waste and wood, rude rocks and level glades,
On thee, on thee I gaze, as Moslems look
To the blest islands of their prophet's book;
And oft I deem that, linked by magic spell,
Pardon and peace upon thy valleys dwell,
Like to sweet houris beckoning o'er the deep
The souls that tremble and the eyes that weep.
Therefore on thee undying sunbeams throw
Their clearest radiance, and their warmest glow;
And tranquil nights, cool gales, and gentle showers
Make bloom eternal in thy sinless bowers.
Green is thy turf; stern Winter doth not dare
To breathe his blast, and leave a ruin there,
And the charmed ocean roams thy rocks around,

With softer motion, and with sweeter sound:
Among thy blooming flowers and blushing fruit
The whispering of young birds is never mute,
And never doth the streamlet cease to well
Through its old channel in the hidden dell.
Oh! if the Muse of Greece had ever strayed,
In solemn twilight, through thy forest shade,
And swept her lyre, and waked thy meads along
The limpid echo of her ancient song,
Her fabling Fancy in that hour had found
Voices of music, shapes of grace, around;
Among thy trees, with merry step and glance,
The Dryad then had wound her wayward dance,
And the cold Naiad in thy waters fair
Bathed her white breast, and wrung her dripping hair.

Beautiful land! upon so pure a plain
Shall Superstition hold her hated reign?
Must Bigotry build up her cheerless shrine
In such an air, on such an earth as thine?
Alas! Religion from thy placid isles
Veils the warm splendour of her heavenly smiles,
And the rapt gazer in the beauteous plan
Sees nothing dark except the soul of Man.

Sweet are the links that bind us to our kind,
Meek, but unyielding,—felt, but undefined;

Sweet is the love of brethren, sweet the joy
Of a young mother in her cradled toy,
And sweet is childhood's deep and earnest glow
Of reverence for a father's head of snow!
Sweeter than all, ere our young hopes depart,
The quickening throb of an impassioned heart,
Beating in silence, eloquently still,
For one loved soul that answers to its thrill.
But where thy smile, Religion, hath not shone,
The chain is riven, and the charm is gone,
And, unawakened by thy wondrous spell,
The feelings slumber in their silent cell.

Hushed is the voice of labour and of mirth,
The light of day is sinking from the earth,
And Evening mantles in her dewy calm
The couch of one who cannot heed its balm.*
Lo! where the chieftain on his matted bed
Leans the faint form, and hangs the feverish head;
There is no lustre in his wandering eye,
His forehead hath no show of majesty,
His gasping lip, too weak for wail or prayer,
Scarce stirs the breeze, and leaves no echo there,

* This sketch of the death of a New Zealander, and of the superstition which prevents the offering of any consolation or assistance, under the idea that a sick man is under the immediate influence of the Deity, is taken from the narrative of the death of Duaterra, a friendly chieftain, recorded by Mr. Nicholas, vol. ii. p. 181.

And his strong arm, so nobly wont to rear
The feathered target, or the ashen spear,
Drops powerless and cold! the pang of death
Locks the set teeth, and chokes the struggling
breath;
And the last glimmering of departing day
Lingers around to herald life away.

Is there no duteous youth to sprinkle now
One drop of water on his lip and brow?
No dark-eyed maid, to bring with soundless foot
The lulling potion, or the healing root?
No tender look to meet his wandering gaze?
No tone of fondness, heard in happier days,
To soothe the terrors of the spirit's flight,
And speak of mercy and of hope to-night?
All love, all leave him!—terrible and slow
Along the crowd the whispered murmurs grow:
"The hand of Heaven is on him! is it ours
"To check the fleeting of his numbered hours?
"Oh, not to us,—oh, not to us is given
"To read the book, or thwart the will, of
Heaven!
"Away, away!" and each familiar face
Recoils in horror from his sad embrace;
The turf on which he lies is hallowed ground,
The sullen priest stalks gloomily around,
And shuddering friends, that dare not soothe or
save,

Hear the last groan, and dig the destined grave.
The frantic widow folds upon her breast
Her glittering trinkets and her gorgeous vest,
Circles her neck with many a mystic charm,
Clasps the rich bracelet on her desperate arm,
Binds her black hair, and stains her eyelid's fringe
With the jet lustre of the Henow's tinge;
Then on the spot where those dear ashes lie,
In bigot transport sits her down to die.
Her swarthy brothers mark the wasted cheek,
The straining eyeball, and the stifled shriek,
And sing the praises of her deathless name,
As the last flutter racks her tortured frame.
They sleep together: o'er the natural tomb
The lichened pine rears up its form of gloom,
And lorn acacias shed their shadow gray,
Bloomless and leafless, o'er the buried clay.
And often there, when, calmly, coldly bright,
The midnight moon flings down her ghastly light,
With solemn murmur, and with silent tread,
The dance is ordered, and the verse is said,
And sights of wonder, sounds of spectral fear,
Scare the quick glance, and chill the startled ear.
Yet direr visions e'en than these remain;
A fiercer guiltiness, a fouler stain!
Oh! who shall sing the scene of savage strife,
Where Hatred glories in the waste of life?

The hurried march, the looks of grim delight,
The yell, the rush, the slaughter, and the flight,
The arms unwearied in the cruel toil,
The hoarded vengeance and the rifled spoil;
And, last of all, the revel in the wood,
The feast of death, the banqueting of blood,
When the wild warrior gazes on his foe,
Convulsed beneath him in his painful throe,
And lifts the knife, and kneels him down to
drain
The purple current from the quiv'ring vein?—
Cease, cease the tale; and let the ocean's roll
Shut the dark horror from my wildered soul!

And are there none to succour? none to speed
A fairer feeling and a holier creed?
Alas! for this, upon the ocean blue,
Lamented Cook, thy pennon hither flew;
For* this, undaunted, o'er the raging brine,
The venturous Frank upheld his Saviour's sign.
Unhappy chief! while Fancy thus surveys
The scattered islets, and the sparkling bays,
Beneath whose cloudless sky and gorgeous sun
Thy life was ended, and thy voyage done,
In shadowy mist thy form appears to glide,
Haunting the grove, or floating on the tide;
Oh! there was grief for thee, and bitter tears,

* From the coast of Australasia the last dispatches of La Peyrouse were dated. Vid. *Quarterly Review*, for Feb. 1810.

And racking doubts through long and joyless
years;
And tender tongues that babbled of the theme,
And lonely hearts that doted on the dream.
Pale Memory deemed she saw thy cherished
form
Snatched from the foe, or rescued from the
storm;
And faithful Love, unfailing and untired,
Clung to each hope, and sighed as each expired.
On the bleak desert, on the tombless sea,
No prayer was said, no requiem sung for thee;
Affection knows not, whether o'er thy grave
The ocean murmur, or the willow wave;
But still the beacon of thy sacred name
Lights ardent souls to Virtue and to Fame;
Still Science mourns thee, and the grateful Muse
Wreathes the green cypress for her own Pey-
rouse.

But not thy death shall mar the gracious plan,
Nor check the task thy pious toil began;
O'er the wide waters of the bounding main
The Book of Life must win its way again,
And in the regions by thy fate endeared,
The Cross be lifted, and the Altar reared.

With furrowed brow and cheek serenely fair,
The calm wind wandering o'er his silver hair,
His arm uplifted, and his moistened eye

Fixed in deep rapture on the golden sky,—
Upon the shore, through many a billow driven,
He kneels at last, the Messenger of Heaven!
Long years, that rank the mighty with the weak,
Have dimmed the flush upon his faded cheek,
And many a dew, and many a noxious damp,
The daily labour, and the nightly lamp,
Have reft away, forever reft, from him,
The liquid accent, and the buoyant limb.
Yet still within him aspirations swell,
Which time corrupts not, sorrow cannot quell:
The changeless Zeal, which on, from land to land,
Speeds the faint foot, and nerves the withered hand,
And the mild Charity, which day by day
Weeps every wound and every stain away,
Rears the young bud on every blighted stem,
And longs to comfort where she must condemn.
With these, through storms, and bitterness, and wrath,
In peace and power he holds his onward path,
Curbs the fierce soul, and sheathes the murd'rous steel,
And calms the passions he hath ceased to feel.

Yes! he hath triumphed!—while his lips relate
The sacred story of his Saviour's fate,
While to the search of that tumultuous horde
He opens wide the Everlasting Word,

And bids the soul drink deep of wisdom there,
In fond devotion, and in fervent prayer,
In speechless awe the wonder-stricken throng
Check their rude feasting and their barbarous song:
Around his steps the gathering myriads crowd,
The chief, the slave, the timid, and the proud;
Of various features, and of various dress,
Like their own forest-leaves, confused and numberless.
Where shall your temples, where your worship be,
Gods of the air, and Rulers of the sea?
In the glad dawning of a kinder light,
Your blind adorer quits your gloomy rite,
And kneels in gladness on his native plain,
A happier votary at a holier fane.

Beautiful Land, farewell!—when toil and strife
And all the sighs, and all the sins of life,
Shall come about me, when the light of Truth
Shall scatter the bright mists that dazzled youth,
And Memory muse in sadness on the past,
And mourn for pleasure far too sweet to last;
How often shall I long for some green spot,
Where, not remembering, and remembered not,
With no false verse to deck my lying bust,
With no fond tear to vex my mould'ring dust,
This busy brain may find its grassy shrine,
And sleep untroubled in a shade like thine!

ATHENS.*

"High towers, faire temples, goodly theaters,
Strong walls, rich porches, princelie pallaces,
Large streetes, brave houses, sacred sepulchers,
Sure gates, sweete gardens, stately galleries,
Wrought with fair pillours and fine imageries,—
All those (O pitie!) now are turned to dust,
And overgrowne with black oblivion's rust."

SPENSER, *The Ruines of Time.*

Muse of old Athens! strike thine ancient lute!
Are the strings broken? is the music mute?
Hast thou no tears to gush, no prayers to flow,
Wails for her fate, or curses for her foe?
If still, within some dark and drear recess,
Clothed with sad pomp and spectral loveliness,
Though pale thy cheek, and torn thy flowing hair,
And reft the roses passion worshipped there,
Thou lingerest, lone, beneath thy laurel bough,
Glad in the incense of a poet's vow,
Bear me, oh, bear me, to the vine-clad hill,
Where Nature smiles, and Beauty blushes still,
And Memory blends her tale of other years
With earnest hopes, deep sighs, and bitter tears!

* This Poem obtained the Chancellor's Medal at the Cambridge Commencement, July, 1824.

Desolate Athens! though thy gods are fled,
Thy temples silent, and thy glory dead,
Though all thou hadst of beautiful and brave
Sleep in the tomb, or moulder in the wave,
Though power and praise forsake thee and forget,
Desolate Athens, thou art lovely yet!
Around thy walls, in every wood and vale,
Thine own sweet bird, the lonely nightingale,
Still makes her home: and when the moonlight hour
Flings its soft magic over brake and bower,
Murmurs her sorrows from her ivy shrine,
Or the thick foliage of the deathless vine.
Where erst Megæra chose her fearful crown,
The bright narcissus hangs his clusters down;
And the gay crocus decks with glittering dew
The yellow radiance of his golden hue.
Still thine own olive haunts its native earth,
Green as when Pallas smiled upon its birth;
And still Cephisus pours his sleepless tide,
So clear and calm, along the meadow side,
That you may gaze long hours upon the stream,
And dream at last the poet's witching dream,
That the sweet Muses, in the neighbouring bowers,
Sweep their wild harps, and wreathe their odorous flowers,
And laughing Venus o'er the level plains
Waves her light lash, and shakes her gilded reins.

How terrible is Time! his solemn years,
The tombs of all our hopes and all our fears,
In silent horror roll!—the gorgeous throne,
The pillared arch, the monumental stone,
Melt in swift ruin; and of mighty climes,
Where Fame told tales of virtues and of crimes,
Where Wisdom taught, and Valour woke to strife,
And Art's creations breathed their mimic life,
And the young Poet, when the stars shone high,
Drank the deep rapture of the quiet sky,
Naught now remains, but Nature's placid scene,
Heaven's deathless blue, and Earth's eternal green,
The showers that fall on palaces and graves,
The suns that shine for freemen and for slaves:
Science may sleep in ruin, man in shame,
But nature lives, still lovely, still the same!
The rock, the river,—these have no decay!
The city and its masters,—where are they?
Go forth, and wander through the cold remains
Of fallen statues, and of tottering fanes,
Seek the loved haunts of poet and of sage,
The gay palæstra, and the gaudy stage!
What signs are there? a solitary stone,
A shattered capital with grass o'ergrown,
A mouldering frieze, half hid in ancient dust,
A thistle springing o'er a nameless bust;—
Yet this *was* Athens! still a holy spell
Breathes in the dome, and wanders in the dell,

And vanished times and wondrous forms appear,
And sudden echoes charm the waking ear:
Decay itself is dressed in glory's gloom,
For every hillock is a hero's tomb,
And every breeze to fancy's slumber brings
The mighty rushing of a spirit's wings.
Oh, yes! where glory such as thine hath been,
Wisdom and Sorrow linger round the scene;
And where the hues of faded splendour sleep,
Age kneels to moralize, and youth to weep!

E'en now, methinks, before the eye of day,
The night of ages rolls its mist away,
And the cold dead, the wise, and fair, and proud,
Start from the urn, and rend the tranquil shroud.
Here the wild Muse hath seized her maddening lyre,
With grasp of passion, and with glance of fire,
And called the visions of her awful reign
From death and gloom, to light and life again.
Hark! the huge Titan on his frozen rock
Scoffs at Heaven's King, and braves the lightning-shock,
The Colchian sorceress drains her last brief bliss,
The thrilling rapture of a mother's kiss,
And the gay Theban raises to the skies
His hueless features, and his rayless eyes.
There blue-eyed Pallas guides the willing feet
Of her loved sages to her calm retreat,

And lights the radiance of her glittering torch
In the rich garden and the quiet porch:
Lo! the thronged arches, and the nodding trees,
Where Truth and Wisdom strayed with Socrates,
Where round sweet Xenophon rapt myriads hung,
And liquid honey dropped from Plato's tongue!
Oh! thou wert glorious then! thy sway and sword
On earth and sea were dreaded and adored,
And Satraps knelt, and Sovereigns tribute paid,
And prostrate cities trembled and obeyed:
The grim Laconian, when he saw thee, sighed,
And frowned the venom of his hate and pride;
And the pale Persian dismal vigils kept,
If Rumor whispered "Athens!" where he slept;
And mighty Ocean, for thy royal sail,
Hushed the loud wave, and stilled the stormy gale;
And to thy sons Olympian Jove had given
A brighter ether, and a purer heaven.
Those sons of thine were not a mingled host,
From various fathers born, from every coast,
And driven from shore to shore, from toil to toil,
To shun a despot, or to seek a spoil;
Oh, no! they drew their unpolluted race
Up from the earth which was their dwelling-place,
And the warm blood, whose blushing streams had run

Ceaseless and stainless, down, from sire to son,
Went clear and brilliant through its hundred rills,
Pure as thy breeze, eternal as thy hills!

Alas! how soon that day of splendour passed,
That bright, brief day, too beautiful to last!
Let other lips tell o'er the oft-told tale;—
How art succeeds, when spear and falchion fail;
How fierce dissension, impotent distrust,
Caprice that made it treason to be just,
And crime in some, and listlessness in all,
Shook the great city to her fate and fall,
Till gold at last made plain the tyrant's way,
And bent all hearts in bondage and decay!
I loathe the task! let other lyres record
The might and mercy of the Roman sword,
The aimless struggle, and the fruitless wile,
The victor's vengeance, and the patron's smile.
Yet, in the gloom of that long, cheerless night,
There gleams one ray to comfort and delight;
One spot of rapture courts the Muse's eye,
In the dull waste of shame and apathy.
Here, where wild Fancy wondrous fictions drew,
And knelt to worship, till she thought them true,—
Here, in the paths which beauteous Error trod,
The great Apostle preached the UNKNOWN GOD!

Silent the crowd were hushed; for his the eye
Which power controls not, sin cannot defy;

His the tall stature, and the lifted hand,
And the fixed countenance of grave command;
And his the voice, which, heard but once, will sink
So deep into the hearts of those that think,
That they may live till years and years are gone,
And never lose one echo of its tone.
Yet, when the voice had ceased, a clamour rose,
And mingled tumult rang from friends and foes;
The threat was muttered, and the galling gibe,
By each pale Sophist and his paltry tribe;
The haughty Stoic passed in gloomy state,
The heartless Cynic scowled his grovelling hate,
And the soft garden's rose-encircled child
Smiled unbelief, and shuddered as he smiled.—
Tranquil he stood; for he had heard,—could hear,
Blame and reproach with an untroubled ear;
O'er his broad forehead visibly were wrought
The dark deep lines of courage and of thought;
And if the colour from his cheek was fled,
Its paleness spoke no passion,—and no dread.
The meek endurance, and the steadfast will,
The patient nerve that suffers, and is still,
The humble faith, that bends to meet the rod,
And the strong hope, that turns from man to God,—
All these were his; and his firm heart was set,
And knew the hour *must* come,—but was not yet.

Again long years of darkness and of pain,
The Moslem scymitar, the Moslem chain;
Where Phidias toiled, the turbaned spoilers brood,
And the Mosque glitters where the Temple stood.
Alas! how well the slaves their fetters wear,
Proud in disgrace, and cheerful in despair!
While the glad music of the boatman's song
On the still air floats happily along.
The light caïque goes bounding on its way
Through the bright ripples of Piræus' bay;
And when the stars shine down, and twinkling feet
In the gay measure blithely part and meet,
The dark-eyed maiden scatters through the grove
Her tones of fondness, and her looks of love:
Oh, sweet the lute, the dance! but bondage flings
Grief on the steps, and discord on the strings;
Yet, thus degraded, sunken as thou art,
Still thou art dear to many a boyish heart;
And many a poet, full of fervour, goes,
To read deep lessons, Athens, in thy woes.
And such was he, the long-lamented one,
England's fair hope, sad Granta's cherished son,
Ill-fated TWEDDELL!—If the flush of youth,
The light of genius, and the glow of truth,
If all that fondness honours and adores,

If all that grief remembers and deplores,
Could bid the spoiler turn his scythe away,
Or snatch one flower from darkness and decay,
Thou hadst not marked, fair city, his decline,
Nor reared the marble in thy silent shrine—
The cold, ungrieving marble—to declare
How many hopes lie desolated there.
We will not mourn for him! ere human ill
Could blight one bliss, or make one feeling chill,
In learning's pure embrace he sunk to rest,
Like a tired child upon his mother's breast;
Peace to his hallowed shade! his ashes dwell
In that sweet spot he loved in life so well,
And the sad Nurse who watched his early
bloom,
From this his home, points proudly to his tomb.

But oft, when twilight sleeps on earth and sea,
Beautiful Athens! we will weep for thee;
For thee, and for thine offspring!—will they
bear
The dreary burden of their own despair,
Till nature yields, and sense and life depart
From the torn sinews and the trampled heart?
Oh! by the mighty shades that dimly glide
Where Victory beams upon the turf or tide,
By those who sleep at Marathon in bliss,
By those who fell at glorious Salamis,
By every laurelled brow and holy name,

By every thought of freedom and of fame,
By all ye bear, by all that ye have borne,
The blow of anger, and the glance of scorn,
The fruitless labour, and the broken rest,
The bitter torture, and the bitterer jest,
By your sweet infant's unavailing cry,
Your sister's blush, your mother's stifled sigh,
By all the tears that ye have wept, and weep,—
Break, Sons of Athens, break your weary sleep!

Yea, it is broken!—Hark, the sudden shock
Rolls on from wave to wave, from rock to rock;
Up, for the Cross and Freedom! far and near
Forth starts the sword, and gleams the patriot spear,
And bursts the echo of the battle-song,
Cheering and swift, the banded hosts along.
On, Sons of Athens! let your wrongs and woes
Burnish the blades, and nerve the whistling bows;
Green be the laurel, ever blest the meed
Of him that shines to-day in martial deed,
And sweet his sleep beneath the dewy sod,
Who falls for fame, his country, and his God!

The hoary sire has helmed his locks of gray,
Scorned the safe hearth, and tottered to the fray;
The beardless boy has left his gilt guitar,
And bared his arm for manhood's holiest war.

E'en the weak girl has mailed her bosom there,
Clasped the rude helmet on her auburn hair,
Changed love's own smile for valour's fiery
glance,
Mirth for the field, the distaff for the lance.
Yes, she was beauteous, that Athenian maid,
When erst she sate within her myrtle shade,
Without a passion, and without a thought,
Save those which innocence and childhood
wrought,
Delicious hopes, and dreams of life and love,
Young flowers below, and cloudless skies above.
But, oh! how fair, how more than doubly fair,
Thus with the laurel twined around her hair,—
While at her feet her country's chiefs assemble,
And those soft tones amid the war-cry tremble,
As some sweet lute creeps eloquently in,
Breaking the tempest of the trumpet's din,—
Her corselet fastened with a golden clasp,—
Her falchion buckled to her tender grasp,—
And quivering lip, flushed cheek, and flashing
eye
All breathing fire, all speaking "Liberty!"

Firm has that struggle been! but is there none
To hymn the triumph, when the fight is won?
Oh for the harp which once—but through the
strings,
Far o'er the sea, the dismal night-wind sings;

Where is the hand that swept it?—cold and mute,
The lifeless master, and the voiceless lute!
The crowded hall, the murmur, and the gaze,
The look of envy, and the voice of praise,
And friendship's smile, and passion's treasured vow,—
All these are nothing,—life is nothing now!
But the hushed triumph, and the garb of gloom,
The sorrow deep, but mute, around the tomb.
The soldier's silence, and the matron's tear,—
These are the trappings of the sable bier,
Which time corrupts not, falsehood cannot hide,
Nor folly scorn, nor calumny deride.
And "what is writ, is writ!"—the guilt and shame,
All eyes have seen them, and all lips may blame;
Where is the record of the wrong that stung,
The charm that tempted, and the grief that wrung?
Let feeble hands, iniquitously just,
Rake up the relics of the sinful dust,
Let Ignorance mock the pang it cannot feel,
And Malice brand, what Mercy would conceal;
It matters not! he died as all would die;
Greece had his earliest song, his latest sigh;
And o'er the shrine, in which that cold heart sleeps,
Glory looks dim, and joyous conquest weeps.

The maids of Athens to the spot shall bring
The freshest roses of the new-born spring,
And Spartan boys their first-won wreath shall bear,
To bloom round BYRON'S urn, or droop in sadness there!

Farewell, sweet ATHENS! thou shalt be again
The sceptred Queen of all thine old domain,
Again be blest in all thy varied charms
Of loveliness and valour, arts and arms.
Forget not then, that in thine hour of dread,
While the weak battled, and the guiltless bled,
Though Kings and Courts stood gazing on thy fate,
The bad, to scoff—the better, to debate,
Here, where the soul of youth remembers yet
The smiles and tears which manhood must forget,
In a far land, the honest and the free
Had lips to pray, and hearts to feel, for thee!

NOTE.—Several images in the early part of the poem are selected from passages in the Greek Tragedians—particularly from the two well-known Choruses in the Œdipus Coloneus and the Medea.

The death of Lord Byron took place after the day appointed for the sending in of the exercises, and the allusion to it was of course introduced subsequently to the adjudication of the prize.

THE ASCENT OF ELIJAH.*

"Ille, feris caput inviolabile Parcis,
Liquit Jordanios turbine raptus, agros."
MILTONI *Lat. Poem.*

SERVANT of God, thy fight is fought;
Servant of God, thy crown is wrought:
Lingerest thou yet upon the joyless earth?
Thy place is now in heaven's high bowers,
Far from this mournful world of ours,
Among the sons of light, that have a different
birth.

Go to the calm and cloudless sphere
Where doubt, and passion, and dim fear,
And black remorse, and anguish have no root;
Turn—turn away thy chastened eyes
From sights that make their tears arise,
And shake th' unworthy dust from thy depart-
ing foot.

Thy human task is ended now;
No more the lightning of thy brow
Shall wake strange terror in the soul of guilt;

* This Poem obtained one of the Seatonian prizes at the University of Cambridge, A. D. 1830.

As when thou wentest forth to fling
The curse upon the shuddering King,
Yet reeking with the blood—the sinless blood he spilt.

And all that thou hast braved and borne,
The Heathen's hate, the Heathen's scorn,
The wasting famine, and the galling chain,—
Henceforth these things to thee shall seem
The phantoms of a bygone dream;
And rest shall be for toil, and blessedness for pain.

Such visions of deep joy might roll
Through the rapt Prophet's inmost soul,
As, with his fond disciple by his side,
He passed with dry and stainless tread
O'er the submissive river's bed,
And took his onward way from Jordan's refluent tide.

High converse held those gifted Seers
Of the dark fates of after years,
Of coming judgments, terrible and fast;
The father's crime, the children's woe,
The noisome pest, the victor foe,
And mercy sealed, and truth made manifest at last.

Thus as they reasoned, hark! on high
Rolled back the portals of the sky;
And from the courts of the empyrean dome
Came forth what seemed a fiery car,
On rushing wheels, each wheel a star,
And bore the Prophet thence,—O whither?—to his home!

With head thrown back, and hand upraised,
Long—long that sad disciple gazed,
As his loved teacher passed for aye away;—
"Alas, my father!" still he cried,
"One look—one word to soothe and guide!—
Chariot and horse are gone from Israel's tents to-day!"

Earth saw the sign;—Earth saw and smiled,
As to her Maker reconciled;
With gladder murmur flowed the streams along;
Unstirred by breath of lightest breeze
Trembled the conscious cedar trees,
And all around the birds breathed gratitude in song.

And viewless harpstrings from the skies
Rang forth delicious harmonies;
And strange, sweet voices poured their grateful hymn;
And radiant eyes were smiling through

The tranquil ether's boundless blue,
The eyes of Heaven's high host, the joyous
Seraphim.

And Piety stood musing by,
And Penitence, with downcast eye;
Faith heard with raptured heart the solemn call,
And, pointing with her lustrous hand
To the far shores of that blest land,
Sent forth her voice of praise,—"for him, O
God,—for all!"

Death frowned far off his icy frown,*
The monarch of the iron crown,
First-born of Sin, the universal foe;
Twice had his baffled darts been vain;
Death trembled for his tottering reign,
And poised the harmless shaft, and drew the idle
bow.

Sons of the Prophets, do ye still
Look through the wood and o'er the hill,
For him, your lord, whom ye may ne'er behold?—
O dreamers, call not him, when day
Fades in the dewy vale away,
Nor when glad morning crests the lofty rocks
with gold!

* "Stassi da un lato Morte furibonda,
Che l'arco ha teso, ed a scoccar s'appresta
Ver la rapita a lei salma seconda—"—*Salomone.*

Peace! call that honoured name no more,
By Jordan's olive-girdled shore,
By Kedron's brook, or Siloa's holy fount;
Nor where the fragrant breezes rove
Through Bethel's dim and silent grove,
Nor on the rugged top of Carmel's sacred mount.

Henceforth ye never more may meet,
Meek learners, at your master's feet,
To gaze on that high brow, those piercing eyes;
And hear the music of that voice,
Whose lessons bade the sad rejoice,
Said to the weak, "Be strong!" and to the dead,
"Arise!"

Go, tell the startled guards that wait
In arms before the palace gate,
"The Seer of Thesbe walks no more on earth:"
The king will bid prepare the feast;
And tyrant prince and treacherous priest
Will move with haughtier step, and laugh with
louder mirth.

And go to Zarephath, and say
What God's right hand hath wrought to-day
To the pale widow and her twice-born son:
Lo, they will weep, and rend their hair,
Upstarting from their broken prayer,—
"Our comforter is gone, our friend, our only
one!"

Nay, deem not so! for there shall dwell
A Prophet yet in Israel
To tread the path which erst Elijah trod;
He too shall mock th' oppressor's spears,
He too shall dry the mourner's tears;
Elijah's robe is his, and his Elijah's God!

But he before the throne of grace
Hath his eternal dwelling-place;
His head is crowned with an unfading crown;
And in the book, the awful book,
On which the angels fear to look,
The chronicle of Heaven, his name is written
down.

Too hard the flight for Passion's wings,
Too high the theme for Fancy's strings;
Inscrutable the wonder of the tale!
Yet the false Sanhedrim will weave
Wild fictions, cunning to deceive,
And hide reluctant Truth in Error's loathly veil.

And some in after years will tell*
How on the Prophet's cradle fell
Rays of rich glory, an unearthly stream;
And some how fearful visions came
Of Israel judged by sword and flame,
That wondrous child the judge, upon his father's
dream.

* See Bayle's Dictionary, Art. "Elijah."

Elijah in the battle's throng
Shall urge the fiery steeds along,
Hurling the lance, lifting the meteor sword:
Elijah, in the day of doom,
Shall wave the censer's rich perfume,
To turn the wrath aside, the vengeance of the Lord.

Vain, vain! it is enough to know
That in his pilgrimage below
He wrought Jehovah's will with steadfast zeal;
And that he passed from this our life
Without the sorrow of the strife
Which all our fathers felt, which we must one day feel.

To us between the world and Heaven
A rougher path, alas! is given;
Red glares the torch, dark waves the funeral pall;
The sceptred king, the trampled slave,
Go down into the common grave,
And there is one decay, one nothingness for all.

It is a fearful thing to die!
To watch the cheerful day flit by
With all its myriad shapes of life and love;
To sink into the dreary gloom
That broods forever o'er the tomb,
Where clouds are all around, though Heaven may shine above!

But still a firm and faithful trust
Supports, consoles the pure and just:
Serene, though sad, they feel life's joys expiro;
And bitter though the death-pang be,
Their spirits through its tortures see
Elijah's car of light, Elijah's steeds of fire.

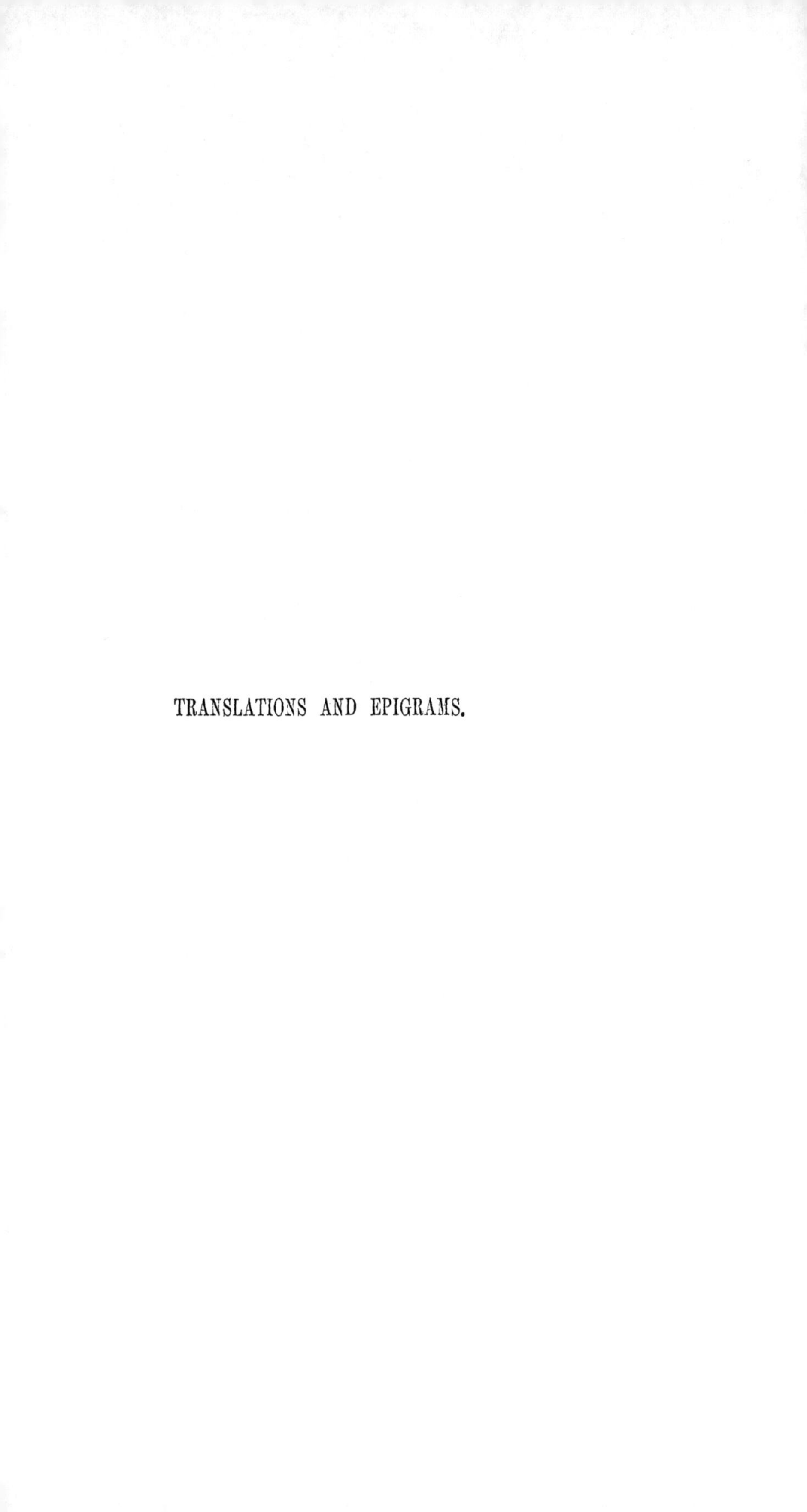

TRANSLATIONS AND EPIGRAMS.

PYRAMIDES ÆGYPTIACÆ.

CARMEN GRÆCUM IN CURIA CANTABRIGIENSI RECITATUM COMITIIS MAXIMIS, A. D. MDCCCXXII.

'ΙΕΡΑΣ ἀγάλματα σεμνὰ γαίας,
ἅσυχοι νεκρῶν θάλαμοι, μέλαθρον
οὐρανοῦ βλέποντες ἀεὶ, παλαιῶν
ἔργα τυράννων,

εἴπατ'—(ἐν γὰρ ὑμετέροις μυχοῖσιν
ἔστιν, ὡς πρὶν, οὐρανία τις αὐδὰ,
μειλίχου λόγον σοφίας βροτοῖς ἅ-
πασιν ἀείδειν)

εἴπαθ' ὡς οὐδὲν διαδήματ', οὐδὲν
γίγνεται σκήπτρων κλέος· ὡς ἅπαντας
λυγρὸν ἁρπάζει σκότος, εὐφρόνη τ' ἄ
ζηλος, ἀτέρμων.

THE PYRAMIDS OF EGYPT.

TRANSLATION OF A GREEK ODE RECITED AT THE CAMBRIDGE COMMENCEMENT, A. D. 1822.

Ye marvels of this ancient land,
  Ye dwellings of the dead,
Where crownèd brow and sceptred hand
  Sleep in their dreamless bed,
Lone monuments of other days
Who lift to Heaven your ceaseless gaze,—

Speak, for within your murky stone
  Philosophy may hear
An echo of a hallowed tone,
  Telling to mortal ear
Lessons of wisdom deep and stern,—
Lessons which pride is slow to learn ;—

Speak how the glory and the power,
  The diadems of kings,
Are but the visions of an hour,
  All unenduring things;
And how that Death hath made for all
A chamber in his silent Hall.

ἴσμεν ὡς βροτοῖσι θανεῖν πέπρωται.
πᾶ τέχνα, πᾶ δ' ἱμερόεν βέβακε
κάλλος ἀνθρώπων; τὸν ἀτέρμον' ὕπνον
εὕδομες ἐν γᾷ.

δυστυχεῖς, ἐφαμέριοι, πτερωτῶν
φάσμ' ὀνειράτων, ὁπόταν σκιαῖσιν
ἀθλίαις ἔλθῃ κεκαλυμμένος δυσ-
έκφυγος Ἀΐδας.

οὐδὲ γὰρ σεμνὰν κεφαλὰν ἄνακτος
χρήμασίν πω πειθόμενος μεθῆκε
Ταρτάρου κευθμών· ὁ δ' ἐν ἀδοναῖς νε-
άνιδος ὥρας

δύσποτμος μέγα φρονέει, τρέφει τε
ἐλπίδων φαῦλον θράσος, ἠδὲ ποσσὶν
μακρὰ βαίνει, κυάνεόν τε θείοις
ὄμμασι λεύσσει,

We know, we know that all must die!
  Where is our knowledge then,—
The plotting head, the beaming eye,
  The boasts of mortal men?
In earth's oblivion, dull and deep,
We sleep our unawakened sleep;

Like forms that float in twilight's shade,
  And ere the day are gone,—
When from his misty, joyless glade
  Stern Hades glideth on,
Wrapped in his robe of quiet gloom,
To call us to the silent tomb.

He will not loose in that dread hour
  The Monarch's jewelled brow,
Won by the wealth, the pomp of power,
  In which he joyeth now;
Poor mortal! while the sun of spring
Smiles on his warm imagining,—

Unhappy!—he hath thoughts of pride,
  And aspirations vain,
And marches with a godlike stride,
  Chilling the courtier train
With the cold glance of royal ire.
More dreaded than the lightning fire.

σχέτλιος· φθίνει τάδε πὰντα, νὺξ γαρ
εἷλεν· ὦ σοφαὶ φρένες, ὦ γελοῖαι
φροντίδες, πόνοι τε· τυραννίκας ἔν-
τοσθε τιάρας

ἱσδάνει, πικρόν τι γελῶν, ὁ λυγρὸς
νερτέρων ἄναξ, Θάνατος· βραχεῖαν δ'
ἁδονὰν χαριζόμενος, κακοῖς γέ-
γαθε δόλοισιν·

αἶψα δ' ὥρμασεν, κρυφίῳ τε κέντρῳ
ἀσθενὲς τεῖχος τόδε χρυσοφεγγὲς
φεῦ διάῤῥηξεν· τί δὲ τίς, τί δ' οὔτις;
νὺξ, ὀλοὴ νὺξ

εἷλε τὸν πρὶν λαμπρότατον, τὸν ἀρχᾶς
ἀγλαὰν ἔχοντα χάριν, τὸν αἰὲν
ἠδ' ἅπαξ εὐδαίμονα, τὸν πανάρχων
ποιμένα λαῶν.

And what are these? in cold and cloud
  The motley pageant flies!
Weep for the weakness of the proud,
  The follies of the wise!
Ever within the golden ring
That rounds the temples of a king,

Death, lord of all beneath the sky,
  Holdeth his stubborn court;
And, as he gives to Royalty
  Its momentary sport,
Points his wan finger all the while
With shaking head, and bitter smile;

And at the last the Phantom thin
  Leaps up within the hold;
And, with a little hidden pin,
  Bores through his wall of gold.
What are we in our fate and fall?—
Night, Night, the jailer of us all,

Hath bound in her funereal chain
  The beautiful, the brave,
The ignorant of human pain,
  The lord of land and wave,
The shepherd of his people's rest,
The ever and the wholly blest.

εὐθὺ δ' ἐν δόμοισῖν ὄρωρε πικρον
οὐλιοῦ γόου νέφος· ἐν δὲ δουπεῖ
(ὡς μάταν) κτύπημα χερῶν· πίτνει δ' ἀ-
μύγματα χαίτας

ἱμέρῳ. λευκὸν δέ δέμας θανόντος
σᾶμα λευκὸν ἐνδέχεται, τυράννων
ὀστέων ἀγανὸν ἕδος, νεκρῶν πε-
λώριον ἕρκος.

ταῦτα μὲν νεκρῶν γέρας ἐστ'. ἐγώ δὲ
εἰσορῶν δῶ μαρμάρεον, παλαιῶν
μνάμαθ' ἡρώων, μύχατ' ἐν σκοτεινᾷ
κείμενα νυκτὶ,

Ψάμμι, σᾶς ἀρχᾶς ἔτι σῶν τε τιμῶν
μνάσομαι· κλυταῖς ἐπέων ἀοιδαῖς
Ψάμμι, σὰν ψυχὰν ἐνὶ νηνέμοις προσ-
φθέγξομαι ὄρφναις.

And straight among the courtier bands
  The hired lamentings rise;
And there is striking of fair hands,
  And weeping of bright eyes;
And the long locks of women fall
In sorrow round that gorgeous Hall.

And last, upon some solemn day,
  The tomb of all his race
Hath opened for his shivering clay
  The dismal dwelling-place,
The dim abyss of sculptured stones,
The prison-house of royal bones.

These are the honours of the dead!
  But, as I wander by,
And gaze upon yon marble bed
  With lost and loitering eye,
Till back upon my awe-struck soul
A thousand ages seem to roll,

I muse on thee, whom this recess
  Hides in its pathless gloom,
Thy glory and thy nothingness,
  Thine empire and thy tomb;
And call thee, Psammis, back to light,
Back from the veil of Death and Night.

ἐλθέ, κικλήσκω σε·—μένεις ἄκλαυστος
μαρμάρῳ πιεζόμενος, δόμον τε
λάϊνον ναίεις·—κροκόβαπτον ἔλθ' εὐ-
μαρὶν ἀείρων,

σκῆπτρον ἐν χείρεσσι λαβὼν, τιάρας
λαμπρὸν ἐκ κρατὸς φάλαρον πιφαύσκων·
ἔλθ', ἄναξ·—σύ μ' οὐκ ἀΐεις·—βέβακας,
Ψάμμι, καὶ ἐν γᾶς

ἀγκάλαις εὕδεις ἔτι, τυμβόχωστόν δ'
ἔργμα πέτραις ἀϊδίοις καλύπτει
σῶμα τοῦ κατοιχομένου, δύσοδμον
σῶμα, τυράννου.

σοὶ δὲ τί χραισμεῖ τάδ'; ὁδοιπόρος τις
τὸν τεὸν σταθήσεται ἀμφὶ τύμβον,
ὀστέων ψυχρὰν σποδιὰν λυθέντων
ποσσὶ πατάσσων·

Come from thy darkness! all too long
  Thou lingerest in the grave;
Thou, the destroyer of the strong,
  The powerful to save:
Come from thy darkness;—set again
Thy saffron sandal on the plain;

And bid thy golden sceptre gleam
  Its wonted radiance yet;
And let thy bright tiara beam
  Around thy locks of jet;
And play the king upon this spot,
As when—alas! thou listenest not!

Thy might hath fleeted from the day;
  Thy very name is hid;
Yet pride hath heaped upon thy clay
  A ponderous Pyramid;
And thou art kingly still, and blest
In a right royal place of rest.

O what is this to thee or thine?
  Some traveller idly stalks
Around the tomb of all thy line,
  And tramples as he walks,
With rebel foot, and reckless eye,
The dust which once was Majesty.

ὅς σ', ἀγακλειτοῖς ποτε μουσοποιῶν
χείρεσιν γεγραμμένον ἐν πελώροις
μνάματος μυχοῖς, ἀπίοισι δείξει
θαῦμα Βρεταννοῖς.

ἦ μάκαρ σὺ, τρὶς μάκαρ· ἀλλ' ἔμοιγε
μηδαμῶς εἴη τόδε σεμνὸν ἄχθος,
μηδαμῶς ἡ χθὼν ὑποκειμένῳ βα-
ρεῖα γένοιτο.

τυτθὸς εἴη μοι τάφος· ἐν βαθείᾳ
κείσομαι βήσσᾳ· μαλακὸς δὶ αὐτᾶς
ἁδὺ φωνάσει Ζέφυρος, καλη τ' ἀ-
εὶ κυπαρίσσῳ

μυρσίνᾳ τε τηλεθόωσα παγὰ
εὔσκιον δεύσει τόπον· ἔνθα πολλὰν
λευκόπεπλος Μναμοσύνα τάφῳ δάφ-
ναν ἐπιθήσει·

Thy portrait and thine eulogy,
  Traced by some artist hand,
And all that now remains of thee,
  Dragged to a distant land,
Must be a thing for girls to know,
A jest, a marvel, and a show!

Hail, happy one!—but not for me,
  So poor, so little worth,
May such a spacious temple be;
  Nor let my mother Earth,
When I am laid in my cold bed,
Lie heavy on my slumbering head:—

Give me a low and humble mound
  In some sequestered dell!
Where Zephyr shall make music round
  My buried dust shall dwell.
There shall the turf with dew be wet;
And while one natural rivulet

Shall wander on its way, and sing
  Beneath the twilight beam,
Cypress and myrtle both shall spring
  Beside its bubbling stream;
And Memory shall scatter there
The laurel I have longed to wear.

πολλάκις δ' ὀδυρομένα ποτέλθοι
σᾶμα τοὐμὸν ἁ τριφίλατος Αἴγλα,—
Χαῖρε, φωνεῦσ' ἀσυχίως, τέρεν τε
δάκρυ χέοισα.

τίς χάρις, τίς, πυραμίδων; ἐμοῦ γὰρ
μνάσεαι σύ· στάθεσιν ἐν τεοῖσιν
ἔσσομαι· φεῦ στάθεσιν ἐν τεοῖσιν
ἔσσομαι, Αἴγλα.

And one fond form shall often glide,
  When tolls the evening bell,
To whisper o'er that tomb and tide
  One echoless " farewell!"
And shed one tear in that dim grove,
The silent tear of parted love.

Raise not for me a Pyramid!
  Carve not a stone for me!
The tear that gleams in that pale lid
  Shall be mine elegy;
And in thy breast, thy tender breast,
My shade shall find a home of rest!

IN OBITUM

VIRI ADMODUM REVERENDI DOCTISSIMIQUE

THOMÆ FANSHAWE MIDDLETON,

EPISCOPI CALCUTTENSIS.

CARMEN GRÆCUM IN CURIA CANTABRIGIENSI RECITATUM
COMITIIS MAXIMIS, A. D. M.DCCC.XXIII.

ΝΑΜΑΤΩΝ πάτερ, βαθύπλουτε Γάγγα,
χαῖρε, χαῖρ' ἐμοί· σὺ μὲν ἐς θάλασσαν
ἁμέρας λαχὼν ἀτέλευτον αὐγὰν
εὔρροον ἱεῖς

κυμάτων κλύδωνα· βλέπων δ' ἐς εὐρὺ
ὠρανῶ μέλαθρον ἀεὶ ποτ' αὔρας
γαρύεις ἀγαλλόμενος μέγαν πο-
λύρροθον ὕμνον.

ἦ μάκαρ σύ· θεσπεσίᾳ γὰρ αὐδᾷ
τὸν Θεὸν τὸν αἰὲν ἀλαθέ' αἰὲν
εὖ σέβεις· παῖδες δὲ τεοὶ κακᾷ κε-
κρυμμένοι ὄρφνᾳ

κεῖνται· ἐν δ' αἰνὸν δέος, ἐν δ' ὄνειδος
βάρβαρον, μῦθοί τε κενοὶ πέτονται·
ἔνθα γὰρ λαῶν φρέν' ἀναλίοις πτυ-
χαῖσι καλύπτε.

HINDOSTAN.

TRANSLATION OF A GREEK ODE TO THE MEMORY OF THE VERY REVEREND AND LEARNED THOMAS FANSHAWE MIDDLETON, BISHOP OF CALCUTTA, RECITED AT THE CAMBRIDGE COMMENCEMENT, A. D. 1823.

FATHER of rivers, Ganges, hail to thee!
Thou, in the joy of thine unfading day,
Goest thy wonted way,
Unwearied, to the sea;

And, ever gazing with a steadfast gaze
On the huge canopy of sunny heaven,
Singest from morn to even
Thy changeless song of praise.

So thou art happy: for thy hymn is loud
Eternally to Him, th' eternal King:
Doubt flaps her murky wing,
Dim Ignorance spreads her cloud

Around thee; and wild fancies, wild and vain,
Hither and thither thread the lurid air:
Darkness, Sin's mother, there
Holds her unlovely reign;

ὁ Σκότος, πυκνὸν νέφος ἀμπετάσσας,
οὐδὲ Φῶς, Θεοῦ τόδε τερπνὸν ἄνθος,
σπαργανωθὲν ἐκ νεφελᾶν καλοὺς βέ-
βακε ποτ' ἀγρούς.
ποσσάκις, φεῦ, ποσσάκις αἱματηρὰς
ἅλιος βλέπει θυσίας;—τίς ὄχλος*
ἔρχεται;—πυρὰν γὰρ ὅρημι κήδει-
όν τε χορείαν
παρθένων, πεπλώματά θ' ἀβρόπηνα,
χρυσίου θ' ἁγνὸν σέλας, ἄργυρόν τε,
βάρβαρον χλίδαμα· μάλ' ἐκφοβεῖται
δῖα Σελάνα
λαμπάδων ὁρῶσα φάος· πάρεστιν
ἁ κόρα· σιγῶσα δίκαν χιμαίρας
κεῖται ἐν τείχει ξυλίνῳ μάταιον
δάκρυ χέοισα.
φεῦ Νεαλλίνα· χλοερὸν γὰρ ἄνθος,
δωμάτων ἄγαλμα, κακῶς ὄλωλεν·
αὐτόχειρ ὄλωλ'· ἱερέων δὲ τέχναι
οὔποτ' ἄκραντοι.

* "Oh sight of grief! the wives of Arvalan,
Young Azla, young Nealliny are seen;
Their widow robes of white,
With gold and jewels bright,
Each like an Eastern queen." . . . . &c.
See SOUTHEY's *Curse of Kehama.*
Canto I. "The Funeral."

And never, since thy glorious course began,
 Hath the glad light, Nature's most precious flower,
 Looked from its home of power
  Upon the soul of Man.

How often yet—how often will the sun
 Behold the rites of death with that calm smile?
 Lo! they have laid the pile;
  The virgins, one by one,

Chant solemnly the hymn—the funeral hymn!
 The rich robes float; the costly gems beam bright;
 The flambeau's flickering light
  Makes the clear day look dim.

Where is the Victim? Lo! the bride appears,
 Mute, motionless, a blameless sacrifice;
 Upon the pile she lies,
  Weeping unheeded tears.

Woe for Nealliny, the tender reed!
 Woe! she has said th' irrevocable vow;—
 Self-slaughtered? Answer thou,
  Priest of a bloody creed!

οἷον ἁ δειλαιοτάτα προβαίνει
οἴμον· ἁ λυγρὰ Παδάλωνος αὐλὰ
νηλεῶς χαίνει, κυανόφρυσιν δ' ὑπ'
ὄμμασι λεύσσει

πικρὸν ὁ στυγνὸς βασιλεύς· παρ' οὐδὲν
αὐχένος ξανθὸν πλόκαμον, παρ' οὐδὲν
χρύσεον λιτῶν μέλος οἱ κακοὶ τί-
θεντι γέροντες·

τυμπάνων ἀχεῖ κέλαδος, συναχεῖ
κύμβαλ'· ἁ δὲ, Χαῖρε, λέγοισα—Χαῖρε,
λείπεται, χεῖλος δ' ἁπαλὸν πυρὸς δι-
έδραμεν ὁρμά.

ταῦτα παρβέβακεν ἀπ' ὀμμάτων· εὖ
παρβέβακε· νῦν δὲ τίς αὐτίκ' ἦνθεν;*
τίς στόνος, τίς; ἆρ' ἀΐεις; ἐν αὔρᾳ
τὰν ἀτέραμνον

ἁρμάτων βροντὰν ἀΐω, καὶ ἀνδρῶν
μυρίων μικτὸν θόρυβον, καὶ ἵππων
θουρίων φρυάγματ'· ἴδ', ὥς πόλιν κυ
λίνδεται ἄμφι

* "Now bring ye forth the chariot of the God!
Bring him abroad,
That through the swarming city he may ride." . . . &c.
See SOUTHEY'S *Curse of Kehama*,
Canto XIV. "Jaga-naut."

For her the dismal pathway must be trod;
The hall of Padalon, the dark, the dread,
Is yawning for its dead,
And the relentless god

Frowns with his moody eyebrows. Naught avail
With those unpitying seers her terrors meek,
Her soft-toned prayers, her cheek
So eloquently pale!

Hark to the cymbal, and the bellowing drum!
"Farewell, farewell!" she whispers.—It is past;
And round her, thick and fast,
The stifling flashes come.

Away, away! they fly, those sights of death.—
Now fiercer echoes scare my shuddering ear!
Hear'st thou? I hear—I hear,
Upon the wild wind's breath,

The thunder of the chariot-wheels, the shout
Of mighty multitudes that cheer or chide,
The charger's voice of pride!—
Hurriedly thronging out

ἐκρέον δόμων ἄπο καὶ ναπάων
κῦμα φωτῶν, ματέρες ἠδὲ παῖδες,
παρθένοι τε πυρσοφοροι· μέσος δ' ὁ
μυριόκρανος

Ὕδρος ὀρθὸς ἡνιοχεῖ, καὶ ὑψοῦ
ἰσδάνων, ἄφαντον ὅραμα, βάκτρον
χρυσέᾳ τείνει χερὶ, λαίνῳ τε
χείλεϊ σαίρει.

ἄξονος δ' ὕπ' ἀργαλέου βρύουσι
φοίνιοι παντᾷ σταγόνες, καὶ ἀχεῖ
ὀστέων δεινὸν πατάγημα· φεῦ, δι'
αἷμα φόνον τε

ἔρχεται Θεοῦ ζυγὸν, οὐδὲ δειλῶν
παύεται βροτῶν ὀλολυγμὸς, οἳ νῦν
ἀθλίῳ πηδήματι τὸν φίλον ζη-
τοῦσιν ὄλεθρον.

ἀμφὶ δὲ στεῤῥὰ τάχ' ὄρωρε φωνά·
Ἄρχεθ' ὕμνων, ἄρχετε· ποικίλοις γὰρ
ἐντὶν ἐν δίφροις ὁ Θεὸς· τὸν αἱμό-
φυρτον ἄνακτα

χρὴ σέβειν. ἰὼ, σέβομεν, στεναγμὸν
εὖ στένοντες θεσπέσιον, χορῷ τε
συγκυκλοῦντες τὸ στεφανηφόρον πε-
λώριον ἅρμα.—

From street and grove the human flood is
poured;
Mothers, and sons, and maidens whose white
hands
Wave wide the blazing brands:
And He, the mighty lord,

The thousand-headed Serpent, sits the while,
Sceptred and crowned, upon his rolling throne,
Writhing his lips of stone
Into a fearful smile.

Beneath the creaking axle the red flood
Gushes unceasing; scattered on the stones
Lie crushed and mangled bones;
Through slaughter and through blood

The chariot of the god—the dark god—reels;
And laughter—shrill, unnatural laughter—
As each mad victim springs [rings
To meet the murderous wheels.

And still the cry goes up: "Begin the song—
Begin!—Behold him on his golden seat,
The terrible! 'tis meet,
Thus as he rides along,

"To worship him, the Lord, whose slaves we are!
Yea, yea, we worship, hymning now the hymn,
And dancing round the grim
And flower-encircled car!"

ἦν ἄρ, ἦν ὢ ταῦτα μέμαλ'· ὄρωρεν,
'Αλβίον, σῶν ἐκ σκοπέλων ὁ σωτὴρ·
ὡς ἴδ', ὡς ἔφριξεν ἰδών· τότ' αὖθις
ἐκ νεφελάων

ποσσὶ λευκοῖς Εὐνομία βὲβακεν,
καὶ κασιγνάτα Δίκα, ἐκπρεπής τε
ἦνθεν Εἰράνα, Θέμιτος θύγατρες
ὀλβοδότειραι.

φεῦ, βραχεῖα τέρψις· ὁ γὰρ τὰ δῶρα
προσφέρων κάλλιστα πατὴρ ὄλωλεν·
κεῖται ἐν νεκροῖσι νεκρός·—θανεῖν βρο-
τοῖσι πέπρωται*

πᾶσιν, εὖ τόδ' οἶδα· καλῶν γε μέντοι
κἀγαθῶν ἔργ' εἰν 'Αΐδα δόμοισιν
ὕστερον ζώοντι, καὶ εἰς ἔτος τάχ'
ἄλλο φύοντι.

εὖ πάθοις, ἄνερ φίλε, κἀν νεκροῖσιν
εὖ πάθοις ἀεί· πεφιλαμένος γὰρ
ἦς ποκ' ἐν ζωοῖς· πεφιλαμένος νῦν
ἔσσεαι ἐν γᾷ·

* "All heads must come
To the cold tomb,
Only the actions of the just
Smell sweet and blossom in the dust."
SHIRLEY.

Is there no help for this lost realm?—from thee,
  My own, my Fatherland, the saviour came;
  He saw the scene of shame—
    He saw, and wept to see.

Soon, at his bidding, Love, the beauteous child,
  Returned; rich Plenty blessed the land's increase;
  Staid Order, gentle Peace,
    Twin-born of Justice, smiled.—

The morrow dawned; and lo! the hand that gave
  Knowledge and mercy forth, is still and cold.
  All men, we know of old,
    Go down into the grave,—

The bad with curses, and the good with tears;
  But still the actions of the pure and just
  Live on, and in the dust
    Bear fruit for other years.

Servant of God, a blessing on thy head!
  E'en in the tomb a blessing! Love did move
  Around thee, living;—Love
    Will not forget thee, dead!

ἔσσεαι· τί πλήν; ὅσιόν γε τύμβον
εὐθέως δαιδάλλομεν, ἐν δέ τύμβῳ.
τὰν τεὰν αἶναν γράφομεν, πόθον τε,
ὦ μακαρῖτα.

ἐνθάδ', εἶδος μαρμάρεον, μάταιον
'Ινδία στένει γόον, αἱ δὲ βᾶσσαι
δειέλοις φύλλων ψιθυρίσμασιν τὰν
πένθιμον αὐδὰν

ἀδέως θρυλλοῦσιν· ὁ δ' ἑπτάφωνος
ὑδάτων πατὴρ βραδὺς ἐς θάλασσαν
κυμάτων χέει ῥόον· ἀσύχῳ κλαί-
ουσα παρ' ὄχθᾳ,

μορσίμοις ἀμαχανέοισα λύπαις,
ἰσδάνει κόρα τις, ἐπὶ ῥεέθροις
ὀμμάτων πήξασα φάος, καλὰς πλέξ-
ασ' ἐνὶ κόλπῳ

ὠλένας·—τοσόνδε γέρας θανόντι
ἁ πατρὶς δίδωσιν, ἀεὶ δ' επ' αὐτῷ
λευκόπαχυς Μναμοσύνα δακρύσει.
τίμιος ἔζης,

εὖ δὲ τέθνακας· πολιὸν γὰρ ὄντα
λαμβάνει σκότος, βιότου τε πόρσω.
εὔχομαι τοιόνδε βίον, πάφον τοι-
όνδε λάχοιμι.

What more than this will Providence allow?
We shape thy monument, and with sad pen
Write, "He was reverenced then,—
He is lamented now!"

There in the living marble India grieves;
The hoary forest seems to send around
A low and wailing sound
From its unnumbered leaves,

And the great River pours its sacred streams
More slowly onward to the mournful sea.
Beneath a spreading tree,
Wrapped in her lonely dreams,

Some maiden sits, pale, with neglected charms,
Hiding a funeral urn within her vest,
And humbly o'er her breast
Folding her snowy arms.

These are thine honours! o'er the hallowed spot,
When the soft moonlight comes upon the vale,
Memory shall tell her tale,
Mourning, and murmuring not;

For silvered o'er with time, and full of days,
Thou sleepest well!—May Heaven to me assign
In life such task as thine,
And in the tomb such praise!

EPIGRAMMATON LIBER:

GRÆCE, LATINE, ANGLICE.

ΕΡΩ ΤΕ ΔΗΤΑ Κ'ΟΥΚ ΕΡΩ.

α΄.

Καρολέττα, πασῶν παρθένων
ὧν οἶδα πουλυ φιλτάτα,
μὴ σφάλλε τὸν φιλοῦντά σε
δόλους πλεκοῦσα μυρίους.
καλεῖς με πρός σε πολλάκις,
φευγεις με τὸν καλούμενον·
φιλάματ' αἰτέοντί μοι
δοῦναι θέλεις τε κοὐ θέλεις·
ἐρᾷν σε φής, σὲ δ' αὐτίκα
οὐ φής·—συ χαῖρε, παρθένων
ὧν οἶδα πουλυ φιλτάτα,
εὕρηκα γὰρ τήνδ' ἔκλυσιν,
εὕρηκα, σῶν αἰνιγμάτων·—
ἐρᾷς με δητα, κοὐκ ἐρᾷς,
ἐρῶ σε δῆτα, κοὐκ ἐρῶ.

(This was one of the Cambridge Prize Epigrams for 1822.)

LOVE AND NO LOVE.

TRANSLATION OF THE FOREGOING.

CHARLOTTE, thou far the dearest belle
  Of all that e'er were dear to me,
Vex not a heart that loves so well
  With such a riddling cruelty!
With softest tone your lips invite,
  And when I come, you haste aside;
You promise me a kiss to-night,
  I take it, and you turn to chide;
You smile,—alas, you frown again;
  You love me,—and you love me not;
I will not shiver Cupid's chain,
  But find a way to loose the knot;
And we an equal flame will prove;
  Love, as you love me, lovely belle,
Love me,—without a spark of love,
  And I will love you—just as well!

β.

Ἀντιβίην μάρναντο καλοῦ περὶ Παρθενοπῆος
  Πάλλας Ἀθηναίη καὶ γλυκύδωρος Ἔρως.
εἶπε δ' Ἀθηναίῃ Παφίας χρυσόπτερος υἱός
  ἄδυ τι πορφυρεοῖς χείλεσι μειδιόων,
εὖγε· τίη δὴ νῶϊ διέσταμεν ἀλλήλοισιν;
  οἶδα γὰρ, ἀμφοτεροῖς παῖς ὅδε δοῦλος ἔφυ.
νεῦσεν Ἀθηναίη· διφύης δ' ἐκ τοῦδε πεφυκώς
  ἀμφοτερῶν τίμας ἄμφεπε Παρθενόπευς.
νῦν γὰρ ἐρᾷ, νῦν δ' οὔ· δοῦλος καὶ ἐλεύθερός ἐστιν·
  ἐστὶν ἄγαν ἄνοος, καὶ σόφος ἐστιν ἄγαν.
πολλάκις ἐξαπίνης σε κατέκφυγεν, ἔκ δὲ παλαίστρας
  πολλάκις ἐξαπίνης ἦνθε τοι, Ἀρσινόη.

γ.

Ἐξοτ' ἔμην ψύχην γλυκεροῖς βάλε Κύπρις ὀϊστοῖς,
  στάθεσιν ἐν μυχατοῖς μύρια τραύματ' ἔχω.
Χλώριδ' ἐρῶ, καὶ Λαΐδ' ἐρῶ, καὶ λάμπρα Κορίννας
  ὄμματα, καὶ μαλάκης χείλε' Ἀναστασίης.
ὤς συ μάταν τόδε τόξον ἔχεις, τάδε, Κύπρι, βέλεμνα
  ὃς γὰρ ἐρῶ πάσας, οὐδεμίαν ποτ' ἐρῶ.

SCRIBIMUS INDOCTI DOCTIQUE.

Οἱ σόφοι οἱ τ' ἄσοφοι πάντες μάλα μουσοποιοῦσιν·
  ἀλλὰ τὸν ἐν τούτῳ κείμενον ἄνδρα τάφῳ
ἢ ἄσοφον καλέειν ἢ χρὴ σοφὸν ἔξοχα πάντων,
  οὐδὲν γὰρ γράψας οἴχεται εἰς 'Αΐδην.
λάμβανε προῖκα, Χάρον, τὸν κουφότατον προσιόντων·
  μοῦνος τῶν θνητῶν οὐ κατάγει κιθάραν.

(This was one of the Cambridge Prize Epigrams for 1824.)

TRANSLATION OF THE FOREGOING.

Both the wise and the witless scribble;
  But the wight, whom here we bury,
    By the grace of the skies
    Must have been very wise,
  Or very foolish,—very!

He never wrote a stanza:
  Small weight will Charon find him;
    The only Ghost
    Who comes to the coast,
  And brings no harp behind him!

NUGÆ SERIA DUCUNT IN MALA.

I.

Odit Charinus serias senum barbas,
Totusque nugis illaborat urbanis.
Nugus amicus, tota territat nutu
Critico theatra, fit gravis cothurnorum
Fidiumque censor, laudat auream Ledæ
Vocem, pedesque mobiles Tigellini,
Et seminudam Thaidos venustatem.
Nugis amicus, scit leves puellarum
Captare risus, ore vota mellito
Garrire callet, seu Neæra seu Phyllis
Telo medullas læserit venenato.
Nugis amicus, per beata Parnassi
Errat vireta, floridas Camenarum
Legit corollas, aureum quatit plectrum,
Permessioque labra proluit rivo.
Quid inde fiet?—his senescit in nugis,
Veneris facetus servus,—et columnarum;
Inutilisque canet, esurit, torpet,
Nimis jocosus, seriusque nugator.

(This was one of the Cambridge Prize Epigrams for 1822.)

TRIFLES END IN SERIOUS EVILS.

TRANSLATION OF THE FOREGOING.

With all a fashionable's rage
Charinus loathes the beard of age;
A trifler all, he loves to sit
The very sovereign of the Pit;
To terrify the Tragic Muse
He talks about the dancers' shoes,
And raves of Vestris' eyes of jet
And Mercandotti's pirouette;
A trifler all, he studies bows,
Makes earnest love in whispered vows,
And talks about the shafts that fly
From Phillis' or Neæra's eye;
A trifler all, he kills an hour
In wandering through Thalia's bower,
Shakes his wild harp with frantic mien,
And gets dead drunk with Hippocrene;
And so becomes an ancient Beau,
The slave of Venus, and the Row;
And prates, and puns, and stares away,
And stupefies from day to day;
Till Death cuts short the quibbling knave,
And sinks the merry—in the Grave!

II.

NUGATOR merus, at nec inficetus,
Tuas, et Veneris, fero catenas.
Nugas mille dabo, dabo libenter,
Gemmas, pallia, Chia vina, pisces,
Pæsti florea serta, serta Pindi.
Nugas mille loquor, loquor disertus,
Preces, blanditias, jocos, amores,
Quotquot sint, Veneres Cupidinesque.
Tu nugas mihi mille conferenti,
Tu nugas mihi mille garrienti,
Compresso memoras, Chloe, susurro
Aras, flammea, nuptias, pudorem,
Et quantum est hominum severiorum.
Aut nugas precor aut nihil! valeto;
Nimis seria, mi Chloe, laboras.

III.

CAVEBIS, Abra, dum Cupidinum curæ
Periculosis te morantur in nugis;
Dum Veneris arma ludicro cies bello,
Nutus, susurros, lacrymas, jocos, risus,
Lyrâque sæpe, sæpe melleo cantu
Formosa mentes implicas reluctantes.
Semper Venus dolosa! serium quiddam
Nugaris, Abra, quæ venusta nugaris.

IV.

Codrus ait, promens epigrammata,—"Nil nisi nugæ!"
Nostra tuæ nugæ sunt mala,—nos legimus.

SCRIBIMUS INDOCTI DOCTIQUE.

I.

Vere novo, quo prata tepent, ardentque poetæ,
Et citharæ, et celeres suave loquuntur aquæ,
Serus Apollinea sternit se Daphnis in umbra,
Et parat intonso thura precesque Deo.
"Phœbe pater, dum tanta cohors te poscit amatque,
Dum rapiunt laurus tot fera labra tuas,—
Dum totoque foro, totoque impune Suburra,
Bacchantur tristes, esuriuntque, chori,—
Dum resonant Aganippeo loca cuncta tumultu,
Templa Deum, montes, antra, macella, casæ,—
Dum nihil est nisi—'cara Venus!'—'formose Cupido!'
Angor, amor, cineres, vulnera, mella, rosæ,—

Quid valeat tanta Daphnin secernere turba?
Unde novo discat Daphnis honore frui?
Quid faciam ut propria decorem mea tempora lauru?
Dic mihi, quid faciam?"—dixit Apollo, "tace!"

(This was one of the Cambridge Prize Epigrams for 1824.)

TRANSLATION OF THE FOREGOING.

The fields in spring were blossoming with poets and with flowers,
And silver streams, and golden dreams, were babbling in the bowers,
When Daphnis lay at close of day within a shady hollow,
And filled the air with smoke and prayer, in honor of Apollo.
"Far-darting King of pipe and string,—while such a host of suits
Are made to thee, unceasingly, for laurels and for lutes,—
While far and wide, on every side, from Bond street to the Fleet,
Some rhyme for praise, and some for bays, and multitudes for meat,—

While verse and prose our feet enclose, whatever scene we search,
In feast, and fair, and market square, in Parliament and church,—
While Paphian smiles, and Cupid's wiles, fill all our ears with vanity,
And rosy chains, and pleasing pains, and fiddles and insanity—
By what new art shall Daphnis start from out the herd of fools?
What wreath or name shall Daphnis claim unheard of in the schools?
What shall I leave, that fame may weave a garland all my own?"
"Leave!" said the God, with fragrant nod,—"Why, leave it all alone!"

II.

Simples and sages
All write in these pages!—
As many a weary witling knows,
I'm Susan's Album! I enclose
Within my green morocco covers
The triflings of a score of lovers,
Roses, lilies, sighings, sadness,
All the armory of madness.
In Susan's Album,—for it's true
That Susan is a little blue,—

All sorts of people rave and rant,
Both those who can, and those who can't;
And Susan smiles on each sweet ditty
In which her witless slaves grow witty,
And says to all her scribbling suitors—
"Queen Venus is the best of tutors!"

TRANSLATIONS.

SONG OF THE SAILORS OF SALAMIS.

(From Sophocles, *Ajax*, v. 596.)

Fair Salamis, the billow's roar
  Wanders around thee yet;
And sailors gaze upon thy shore
  Firm in the ocean set.
Thy son is in a foreign clime
  Where Ida feeds her countless flocks,
  Far from thy dear remembered rocks,
Worn by the waste of time,—
Comfortless, nameless, hopeless,—save
In the dark prospect of the yawning grave.

And Ajax, in his deep distress
  Allied to our disgrace,
Hath cherished in his loneliness
  The bosom friend's embrace.

Frenzy hath seized thy dearest son,
Who from thy shores in glory came
The first in valour and in fame;
The deeds that he hath done
Seem hostile all to hostile eyes;
The sons of Atreus see them, and despise.

Woe to the mother, in her close of day,
Woe to her desolate heart, and temples gray,
When she shall hear
Her loved one's story whispered in her ear!
"Woe, woe!" will be the cry,—
No quiet murmur, like the tremulous wail
Of the lone bird, the querulous nightingale,—
But shrieks that fly
Piercing, and wild, and loud, shall mourn the tale;
And she will beat her breast and rend her hair,
Scattering the silver locks that time hath left her there.

Oh! when the pride of Græcia's noblest race
Wanders, as now, in darkness and disgrace,
When Reason's day
Sets rayless—joyless—quenched in cold decay,
Better to die, and sleep
The never-waking sleep, than linger on,
And dare to live, when the soul's life is gone;
But thou shalt weep,

Thou wretched father, for thy dearest son,
Thy best beloved, by inward Furies torn,
The deepest, bitterest curse, thine ancient house
hath borne!

(November 29, 1821.)

THE DEATH OF AJAX.*

(From Ovid's *Metamorphoses.*)

The Kings were moved; conviction hung
On soft Persuasion's honeyed tongue;
And Victory to Wisdom gave
The weapons of the fallen brave.

That Chief, unshrinking, unsubdued,
Had grasped his spear in fire and feud,
And never dreamed of fear;
Had stemmed fierce Hector's wild alarm,—
Had braved the Thunderer's red right arm,—
But Rage is Victor here.
By nothing could the hero fall
Save by the pangs that conquer all!

* This and the two succeeding pieces were written in a College Examination.

He snatched the falchion from his side;
And, "This at least is mine," he cried,
"This e'en Ulysses will not crave:
But let it dig its master's grave:
In many a glorious field of yore
This blade has blushed with Phrygian gore,
And when mine own shall glisten, mine
Shall well become its warlike shine.
Ajax shall fall by Ajax' hand,
A warrior by a warrior's brand."

He spoke, and smiling sternly, pressed
The weapon to his struggling breast.
Too feeble was the hero's strength
To force the weapon's chilling length
  From out the reeking wound;
The blood upon its gory track
In rushing eddies bore it back;
  And on the moistened ground
There bloomed (as poets love to tell),
Where'er the gushing dewdrops fell,
  A melancholy Flower;
The same fair flower had wept beside
The turf where Hyacinthus died;
  And, from that fatal hour,
It syllables on every leaf
The record of a double grief.

(May, 1822.)

ÆNEAS AND THE SIBYL.

(From VIRG. *Æn.* vi. 255.)

BUT look, where first the God of Day
From Heaven pours out his golden ray,
   Earth groans a sullen groan;
Shake the old monarchs of the woods,
And ban-dogs from their solitudes
   Shriek out their ominous moan.
"Avaunt!" the shuddering Sibyl cries,
"Avaunt, ye unpermitted eyes!
And thou, Æneas, twine thine hand,
Fearless, around thy ready brand,
   And come in darkness on!"
She spoke, and through the cavern led:
He followed with as firm a tread.

They went, unseen, through cold and cloud,
Where Darkness flung her solemn shroud—
   A dim, unearthly shade:
Mirk was the air, as when through night
The moon looks down with partial light,
When Jupiter to earth and heaven
A drear and viewless veil hath given,
And, in the calm obscure of even,
   All things and colours fade.

"Ye Gods, whom destiny hath made
The Guardians of the voiceless shade,—
The voiceless shade of parted souls,
Where Phlegethon forever rolls,
  And gloomy Chaos reigns,—
Forgive me that with living eye
I look upon your privacy,
And rend the sulphurous canopy
  Which clothes your dark domains!"

(May, 1822.)

THE HOOPOE'S INVOCATION TO THE NIGHTINGALE.

(From the *Birds* of Aristophanes, l. 209.)

Waken, dear one, from thy slumbers;
Pour again those holy numbers,
Which thou warblest there alone
In a heaven-instructed tone,
Mourning from this leafy shrine
Lost—lost Itys, mine and thine,
In the melancholy cry
Of a mother's agony;
Echo, ere the murmurs fade,
Bears them from the yew-tree's shade

To the throne of Jove; and there,
Phœbus with his golden hair
Listens long, and loves to suit
To his ivory-mounted lute
Thy sad music;—at the sound
All the gods come dancing round,
And a sympathetic song
Peals from the immortal throng.

(SEPTEMBER, 1826.)

FROM LUCRETIUS, Bk. ii. l 1–33.

OH, sweet it is to listen on the shore
When the wild tempest mocks the seaboy's cry;
And sweet to mark the tumult and the roar
When distant battle stalks in thunder by;
And do not say another's agony
Is happiness to us!—oh, rather deem
That the mind loves, in its own fantasy,
To wield the weapons and to scream the scream,
And then to wake from death, and feel it was a dream.

But naught is sweeter than to hold our state,
Unchangeable, on Wisdom's guarded keep,
And look in silence on the low and great,
Who, in their sackcloth or their purple, creep
Beneath the summit of the viewless steep:
They dare the deserts, and they tempt the waves,
And serve, and monarchize, and laugh and weep,
While Fortune scoffs alike at lords and slaves,
And decks the perilous path with sceptres, and with graves.

Oh, wretched souls! oh, weak and wasted breath,
Painful in birth, and loathsome in decay!
Eternal clouds are round us: doubt and death
Lie dark between to-morrow and to-day;
And thus our span of mourning flits away!
If the veins glisten and the pulses glow,
If the free spirits innocently play,
Say, wilt thou seek for more? vain mortal, no!
What more can Dust demand, or Destiny bestow?

Yet Nature hath more blessings, her own joys,
Unearned by labour, and unsought by prayer:
Be wise to-day!—perhaps no golden boys
O'er the thronged banquet fling the torches' glare,

No rich aroma loads the languid air,
No burnished silver gleams along the hall
In dazzling whiteness, no fond lute is there
To wreathe the sweetness of its magic thrall
O'er listening ears, rapt hearts, at some high festival;—

Yet Nature's fondest sons and fairest daughters
On her green bosom love at eve to lie,
Where the lone rippling of the quiet waters
Goes syllabling all sweets, and hoar and high
The old oak lends his solemn canopy.
What do they reck beneath their tranquil bowers
Of guilt or grief?—then happiest, when the sky
Laughs in the glad spring-dawning, and the hours
Dress every hill and vale in herbs and odorous flowers!

(1826.)

STANS PEDE IN UNO.

——καὶ νῦν ἐν Ἄρεϊ
μαρτυρῆσαι κεν πόλις Αἴ-
αντος ὀρθωθεῖσα ναύταις
ἐν πολυφθόρῳ Σαλάμις Διὸς ὄμβρῳ.
Pindar, Isth. v. 61.

NOVENA Pindi turba, licet Jovis
Antiqua cessent fulmina vatibus
  Mentita, Divorumque voces
    Per vacuum taceant Olympum,

At usque clivo vos Heliconio
Ludum vetustum ludite, vos aquas
  Libate sollennes, lyrarum
    Vos dominæ dominæque vatum

Audite! Nymphæ Pierides, quibus
Cordi est celebres martis honoribus
  Ornare reges, et triumphos
    Aonio resonare plectro,

Vos a quietis vos mihi montibus
Adeste, Nymphæ! ferte per inclytas
  Urbes, et antiqua sacratos
    Relligione domos; juvabit

Cælestibus fervere furoribus,
Juvabit umbras inter et abditos
  Errare Manes, quos perennis
    Ambit Honor, meritæque laudis

Corolla. Fallorne an videor tua
Solers Ulysseu mœnia? non latet
  Larissa, non Spartana pubes,
    Non Agamemnoniæ Mycenæ.

Insanientes territus audio
Fluctus Athenarum; haurio amabilem
  Sublimis auram; lentiori
    Pervolito Salamina pennâ;

Inter frementes Oceani minas
Dirosque ventos usque morabitur
  Dilecta Musarum choreis
    Insula, perpetuâque lauru

Insignis, ex quo cedere nescium
Heroa celsum misit in Ilium
  Quem Fama quem palmæ decorus
    Egit Amor per acuta belli.

Non ille cara pro patria necem
Obire segnis, cum furiosior
  Omnis super Graias volaret
    Troja rates: furit inter arma

Interque cædes Hector, et horrido
Clamore vires deficientium
  Invictus accendit—"Quid atri
    Martis opus trepidabit olim

Trojana virtus? ibitis, ibitis,
Fortes amici, per medias neces
  Utcunque præcedant secundi
    Signa Jovis; jacet ille tandem

Audax Achilles, et sapientior
Tuto latescit mersus in otio:
  Incumbite hosti! jam decoro
    Nec mora nec requies labori

Donec labantes Grajugenum rates
Incensa late flamma voraverit,
  Vastumque Neptuni barathrum
    Sorpserit Argolicos latrones."

(1822.)

SONGS.

LORD ROLAND.

Lord Roland rose, and went to mass,
And doffed his mourning weed;
And bade them bring a looking-glass,
And saddle fast a steed;
I'll deck with gems my bonnet's loop,
And wear a feather fine,
And when lorn lovers sit and droop,
Why, I will sit and dine;—
Sing merrily, sing merrily!
And fill the cup of wine.

Though Elgitha be thus untrue,
Adèle is beauteous yet;
And he that's baffled by the blue
May bow before the jet;
So welcome, welcome, hall or heath!
So welcome, shower or shine!
And wither there, thou willow wreath,
Thou never shalt be mine;—
Sing merrily, sing merrily!
And fill the cup of wine.

Proud Elgitha! a health to thee,
A health in brimming gold,

And store of lovers after me,
As honest, and less cold;
My hand is on my bugle-horn,
My boat is on the brine;
If ever gallant died of scorn
I shall not die of thine;—
Sing merrily, sing merrily!
And fill the cup of wine.

(1824.)

YES OR NO.

I.

The Baron de Vaux hath a valiant crest,—
My Lady is fair and free;
The Baron is full of mirth and jest,—
My Lady is full of glee;
But their path, we know, is a path of woe,
And many the reason guess,—
The Baron will ever mutter "No,"
When my Lady whispers "Yes.'

II.

The Baron will pass the wine-cup round,—
My Lady forth will roam;
The Baron will out with horse and hound,—
My Lady sits at home;

The Baron will go to draw the bow,
  My Lady will go to chess;
And the Baron will ever mutter "No,"
  When my Lady whispers "Yes."

III.

The Baron hath ears for a lovely lay,
  If my Lady sings it not;
The Baron is blind to a beauteous day,
  If it beam in my Lady's grot;
The Baron bows low to a furbelow,
  If it be not my Lady's dress;
And the Baron will ever mutter "No,"
  When my Lady whispers "Yes."

IV.

Now saddle my steed, and helm my head,
  Be ready in the porch;
Stout Guy, with a ladder of silken thread,
  And trusty Will, with a torch:
The wind may blow, the torrent flow,
  No matter,—on we press;
I never can near the Baron's "No,"
  When my Lady whispers "Yes."

(1827.)

TELL HIM I LOVE HIM YET.

I.

Tell him I love him yet,
  As in that joyous time;
Tell him I ne'er forget,
  Though memory now be crime;
Tell him, when sad moonlight
  Is over earth and sea,
I dream of him by night,—
  He must not dream of me!

II.

Tell him to go where Fame
  Looks proudly on the brave;
Tell him to win a name
  By deeds on land and wave;
Green, green upon his brow
  The laurel wreath shall be;
Although the laurel now
  May not be shared with me.

III.

Tell him to smile again
  In Pleasure's dazzling throng,
To wear another's chain,
  To praise another's song;

Before the loveliest there
  I'd have him bend his knee,
And breathe to her the prayer
  He used to breathe to me.

IV.

And tell him, day by day,
  Life looks to me more dim;
I falter when I pray,
  Although I pray for him;
And bid him, when I die,
  Come to our favourite tree;
I shall not hear him sigh,—
  Then let him sigh for me!

(July 20, 1829.)

WHERE IS MISS MYRTLE?

Air—"Sweet Kitty Clover."

I.

Where is Miss Myrtle? can any one tell?
  Where is she gone, where is she gone?
She flirts with another, I know very well,
  And—I am left alone!
She flies to the window when Arundel rings,—

She's all over smiles when Lord Archibald sings,—
It's plain that her Cupid has two pair of wings:
  Where is she gone, where is she gone?
Her love and my love are different things;
  And I—am left all alone!

II.

I brought her, one morning, a rose for her brow;
  Where is she gone, where is she gone?
She told me such horrors were never worn now;
  And I—am left all alone!
But I saw her at night with a rose in her hair,
And I guess who it came from—of course I don't care!
We all know that girls are as false as they're fair;
  Where is she gone, where is she gone?
I'm sure the lieutenant's a horrible bear,
  And I—am left all alone!

III.

Whenever we go on the Downs for a ride,—
  Where is she gone, where is she gone?
She looks for another to trot by her side:
  And I—am left all alone!
And whenever I take her down stairs from a ball,
She nods to some puppy to put on her shawl:
I'm a peaceable man, and I don't like a brawl;—
  Where is she gone, where is she gone?

But I would give a trifle to horsewhip them all;
And I—am left all alone!

IV.

She tells me her mother belongs to the sect,—
Where is she gone, where is she gone?
Which holds that all waltzing is quite incorrect:
And I—am left all alone!
But a fire's in my heart, a fire's in my brain,
When she waltzes away with Sir Phelim O'Shane;
I don't think I ever *can* ask her again:
Where is she gone, where is she gone?
And, Lord! since the summer she's grown very plain;
And I—am left all alone!

V.

She said that she liked me a twelvemonth ago;
Where is she gone, where is she gone?
And how should I guess that she'd torture me so?
And I—am left all alone!
Some day she'll find out it was not very wise
To laugh at the breath of a true lover's sighs;
After all, Fanny Myrtle is not such a prize:
Where is she gone, where is she gone?—
Louisa Dalrymple has exquisite eyes;
And I'll be no longer alone!

(1831.)

THE CONFESSION.

I.

FATHER—Father—I confess—
Here he kneeled and sighed,
When the moon's soft loveliness
Slept on surf and tide.
In my ear the prayer he prayed
Seems to echo yet;
But the answer that I made—
Father—I forget!
Ora pro me!

II.

Father—Father—I confess—
Precious gifts he brought;
Satin sandal, silken dress;
Richer ne'er were wrought;
Gems that make the daylight dim,
Plumes in gay gold set;—
But the gaud I gave to him—
Father—I forget!
Ora pro me!

III.

Father—father—I confess—
He's my beauty's thrall,
In the lonely wilderness,
In the festive hall;
All his dreams are aye of me,
Since our young hearts met;
What my own may sometimes be—
Father—I forget!
Ora pro me!

LAST WORDS.

I.

Fare thee well, love,—fare thee well!
From the world I pass away,
Where the brightest things that dwell
All deceive, and all decay;
Cheerfully I fall asleep,
As by some mysterious spell;
Yet I weep, to see thee weep;
Fare thee well, love,—fare thee well!

II.

Tell of me, love, tell of me!
  Not amid the heartless throng;
Not where Passion bends the knee,—
  Not where Pleasure trills the song,
But when some most cherished one
  By your side at eve shall be,
Ere your twilight tales are done,
  Tell of me, love,—tell of me!

III.

Leave me now, love,—leave me now
  Not with sorrow, not with sighs;
Not with clouds, love, on thy brow,
  Not with tears, love, in thine eyes;
We shall meet, we know not where,
  And be blest, we dream not how;
With a kiss, and with a prayer,
  Leave me now, love,—leave me now!

(April, 1832.)

THE RUNAWAY.

I.

Dark clouds are shading
  The day,—the day;
Sunlight is fading
  Away,—away;
I've won from the warden
  The key,—the key,
And the steed's in the garden
  For me,—for me.

II.

Locks of my mother,
  So white,—so white,—
Frowns of my father,
  Good night,—good night!
From turret and tower
  I'm free,—I'm free,
And your rage has no power
  O'er me,—o'er me.

III.

Shriller is grieving
  The blast,—the blast;
Lo, the waves heaving
  At last,—at last!

'Twas here he, the bold one,
  Should be,—should be;
And lingers he, cold one!
  Ah, me!—ah, me!

IV.

Vain is thy chiding,
  For hark!—for hark!
Hither 'tis gliding,
  The bark!—the bark!
Joyously over
  The sea,—the sea,
She'll waft my brave lover
  With me,—with me!

(April, 1882.)

LONG AGO.

I.

We were children together! Oh, brighter than mine
  Are the eyes that are looking their love on you now;
And nobler than I are the maidens that twine
  The scarf for your breast, and the wreath for your brow.

Be happy, my brother, wherever you will;
  Good speed to your courser, good luck to your bow;
But will you not—will you not think of me still,
  As you thought of me once,—long ago—long ago?

II.

We were children together! I know you will dream
  Of the rock and the valley, the cottage and tree;
Of the bird on the brake, of the boat on the stream,
  Of the book and the lute, of my roses and me;
When Pleasure deceives you, and young Hope departs,
  And the pulse of Ambition beats weary and low,
My brother—my brother—come back to our hearts:
  Let us be what we were,—long ago—long ago!

(August, 1832.)

I REMEMBER, I REMEMBER.

I.

I remember—I remember
  How my childhood fleeted by,—
The mirth of its December,
  And the warmth of its July;
On my brow, love—on my brow, love,
  There are no signs of care;
But my pleasures are not now, love,
  What Childhood's pleasures were.

II.

Then the bowers—then the bowers
  Were blithe as blithe could be;
And all their radiant flowers
  Were coronals for me:
Gems to-night, love—gems to-night, love,
  Are gleaming in my hair;
But they are not half so bright, love,
  As Childhood's roses were.

III.

I was singing—I was singing,
  And my songs were idle words;
But from my heart was springing
  Wild music like a bird's:

Now I sing, love—now I sing, love,
  A fine Italian air;
But it's not so glad a thing, love,
  As Childhood's ballads were!

IV.

I was merry—I was merry
  When my little lovers came,
With a lily, or a cherry,
  Or a new-invented game;
Now I've you, love—now I've you, love,
  To kneel before me there;
But you know you're not so true, love,
  As Childhood's lovers were!

(June, 1833.)

SHADOWS OF SADNESS.

I.

Shadows of sadness
  Come o'er thy young bride;
They cloud all her gladness,
  They calm all her pride;
A bright home I leave, love;
  From dear friends I fly;
In bliss I must grieve, love;
  In bliss let me sigh!

II.

On the green bowers
  That echoed my song,—
On all the glad flowers
  I cherished so long,—
On yon merry brook, love,
  In light gushing by,
I look my last look, love;
  For these let me sigh!

III.

There my gay brother
  Less joyous is grown;
And there my fond mother
  Sits pensive and lone;
Roam—rest where I will, love,
  Beneath a fair sky,
They'll sigh for me still, love;
  For them let me sigh!

IV.

Though I forget not
  The name I bear now,
And though I regret not
  The ring or the vow,
A cloud's on my heart, love,
  A tear's in mine eye;
Most dear as thou art, love,
  To-day let me sigh!

(December 16, 1836.)

CHARADES AND ENIGMAS.

CHARADES AND ENIGMAS.*

I.

The First is for love and thee, Mary,—
  The First is for love and thee;
    And so firmly hold
    Those links of gold,
That the Second it never shall be—Mary!

The Second is ever free, Mary,—
  Free as the foaming brine;
    As the fires that fly
    From the poet's eye,
Or the laugh that speaks in thine—Mary!

Though the First be a wayward thing, Mary,—
  Though a wayward thing it be,
    When thought hath power
    In the midnight hour,
Be sure it is ever with thee—Mary!

* Should the solutions be required, they will be found given in the Table of Contents to this volume.

II.

ENIGMA.

THROUGH thy short and shadowy span
I am with thee, Child of Man;
With thee still, from first to last,
In pain and pleasure, feast and fast,
At thy cradle and thy death,
Thine earliest wail, and dying breath.
Seek not thou to shun or save,
On the earth, or in the grave;
The worm and I, the worm and I,
In the grave together lie.

(NOVEMBER, 1821.)

III.

Sir Hilary charged at Agincourt,—
  Sooth 'twas an awful day!
And though in that old age of sport
The rufflers of the camp and court
  Had little time to pray,
'Tis said Sir Hilary muttered there
Two syllables by way of prayer.

My First to all the brave and proud
  Who see to-morrow's sun;
My Next with her cold and quiet cloud
To those who find their dewy shroud
  Before to-day's be done;
And both together to all blue eyes
That weep when a warrior nobly dies.

IV.

ENIGMA.

A Templar kneeled at a friar's knee;
He was a comely youth to see,
With curling locks and forehead high,
And flushing cheek, and flashing eye;
And the monk was as jolly and large a man
As ever laid lip to a convent can,
        Or called for a contribution—
As ever read, at midnight hour,
Confessional in lady's bower,
Ordained for a peasant the penance whip,
Or spoke for a noble's venial slip
        A venal absolution.

"Oh, Father! in the dim twilight
I have sinned a grievous sin to-night;
And I feel hot pain e'en now begun
For the fearful murder I have done.

"I rent my victim's coat of green;
I pierced his neck with my dagger keen;
        The red stream mantled high;

I grasped him, Father, all the while
With shaking hand, and feverish smile,
And said my jest, and sang my song,
And laughed my laughter, loud and long,
        Until his glass was dry!

"Though he was rich, and very old,
I did not touch a grain of gold,
But the blood I drank from the bubbling vein
Hath left on my lip a purple stain."

"My son! my son! for this thou hast dōne,
Though the sands of thy life for aye should run,"
        The merry monk did say;
"Though thine eye be bright, and thine heart
        be light,
Hot spirits shall haunt thee all the night,
        Blue devils all the day."

The thunders of the Church were ended,
Back on his way the Templar wended;
But the name of him the Templar slew
Was more than the Inquisition knew.

V.

My First, in torrents bleak and black,
  Was rushing from the sky,
When, with my Second at his back,
  Young Cupid wandered by:
"Now take me in; the moon hath passed;
  I pray ye, take me in!
The lightnings flash, the hail falls fast,
All Hades rides the thunder-blast;
  I'm dripping to the skin!"

"I know thee well, thy songs and sighs;
  A wicked god thou art,
And yet most welcome to the eyes,
  Most witching to the heart!"
The wanderer prayed another prayer,
  And shook his drooping wing;
The lover bade him enter there,
And wrung my First from out his hair,
  And dried my Second's string.

And therefore—(so the urchin swore,
  By Styx, the fearful river,
And by the shafts his quiver bore,
  And by his shining quiver),

That Lover aye shall see my whole
  In Life's tempestuous Heaven;
And when the lightnings cease to roll,
Shall fix thereon his dreaming soul
  In the deep calm of even!

VI.

The Indian lover burst
  From his lone cot by night;—
When Love hath lit my First,
In hearts by Passion nursed,
  Oh! who shall quench the light?

The Indian left the shore;
  He heard the night wind sing,
And cursed the tardy oar,
And wished that he could soar
  Upon my Second's wing.

The blast came cold and damp,
  But, all the voyage through,
I lent my lingering lamp,
As o'er the marshy swamp
  He paddled his canoe.

VII.

ENIGMA.

In other days, when hope was bright,
Ye spake to me of love and light,
Of endless spring, and cloudless weather,
And hearts that doted linked together!

But now ye tell another tale,—
That life is brief, and beauty frail,
That joy is dead, and fondness blighted,
And hearts that doted disunited!

Away! ye grieve and ye rejoice
In one unfelt, unfeeling voice;
And ye, like every friend below,
Are hollow in your joy and woe!

VIII.

Alas! for that forgotten day
  When Chivalry was nourished,
When none but friars learned to pray,
  And beef and beauty flourished!
And fraud in kings was held accursed,
  And falsehood sin was reckoned,

And mighty chargers bore my First,
  And fat monks wore my Second!

Oh, then I carried sword and shield,
  And casque with flaunting feather,
And earned my spurs in battle-field,
  In winter and rough weather;
And polished many a sonnet up
  To ladies' eyes and tresses,
And learned to drain my father's cup,
  And loose my falcon's jesses:

How grand was I in olden days!
  How gilded o'er with glory!
The happy mark of ladies' praise,
  The theme of minstrel's story:
Unmoved by fearful accidents,
  All hardships stoutly spurning,
I laughed to scorn the elements—
  And chiefly those of Learning.

Such things have vanished like a dream;
  The mongrel mob grows prouder;
And every thing is done by steam,
  And men are killed by powder;
I feel, alas! my fame decay;
  I give unheeded orders,
And rot in paltry state away,
  With Sheriffs and Recorders.

IX.

My First's an airy thing,
  Joying in its flowers,
Evermore wandering
  In Fancy's bowers;
Living on beauteous smiles
  From eyes that glisten,
And telling of Love's wiles
  To ears that listen.

But if, in its first flush
  Of warm emotion,
My Second come to crush
  Its young devotion,
Oh! then it wastes away,
  Weeping and waking,
And on some sunny day,
  Is blest in breaking.

X.

ON the casement frame the wind beat high,
Never a star was in the sky;
All Kenneth Hold was wrapt in gloom,
And Sir Everard slept in the Haunted Room.

I sat and sang beside his bed;
Never a single word I said,
Yet did I scare his slumber;
And a fitful light in his eye-ball glistened,
And his cheek grew pale as he lay and listened,
For he thought, or he dreamed, that fiends and fays
Were reckoning o'er his fleeting days,
And telling out their number.
Was it my Second's ceaseless tone?
On my Second's hand he laid his own:
The hand that trembled in his grasp
Was crushed by his convulsive clasp.

Sir Everard did not fear my First;
He had seen it in shapes that men deem worst,
In many a field and flood;
Yet, in the darkness of that dread,
His tongue was parched, and his reason fled;

And he watched as the lamp burned low and
dim,
To see some Phantom, gaunt and grim,
Come, dabbled o'er with blood.

Sir Everard kneeled, and strove to pray;
He prayed for light, and he prayed for day,
Till terror checked his prayer;
And ever I muttered, clear and well,
"Click, click," like a tolling bell,
Till, bound by Fancy's magic spell,
Sir Everard fainted there.

And oft, from that remembered night,
Around the taper's flickering light
The wrinkled beldames told,
Sir Everard had knowledge won
Of many a murder darkly done,
Of fearful sights and fearful sounds,
And Ghosts that walk their midnight rounds
In the Tower of Kenneth Hold!

(1822.)

XI.

THE canvas rattled on the mast,
  As rose the swelling sail;
And gallantly the vessel passed
  Before the cheering gale;
And on my First Sir Florice stood,
  As the far shore faded now,
And looked upon the lengthening flood
  With a pale and pensive brow:
"When I shall bear thy silken glove
  Where the proudest Moslem flee,
My lady love, my lady love,
  Oh, waste one thought on me!"

Sir Florice lay in a dungeon cell,
  With none to soothe or save;
And high above his chamber fell
  The echo of the wave;
But still he struck my Second there,
  And bade its tones renew
Those hours when every hue was fair,
  And every hope was true:—
"If still your angel footsteps move,
  Where mine may never be,

My lady love, my lady love,
  Oh, dream one dream of me!"

Not long the Christian captive pined!—
  My Whole was round his neck;
A sadder necklace ne'er was twined,
  So white a skin to deck;
Queen Folly ne'er was yet content
  With gems or golden store,
But he who wears this ornament,
  Will rarely sigh for more;—
"My spirit to the Heaven above,
  My body to the sea,
My heart to thee, my lady love,
  Oh, weep one tear for me!"

XII.

Row on, row on!—The First may light
My shallop o'er the wave to-night;
But she will hide in a little while,
The lustre of her silent smile;
For fickle she is, and changeful still,
As a madman's wish, or a woman's will.

Row on, row on!—The Second is high
In my own bright lady's balcony;
And she beside it, pale and mute—
Untold her beads, untouched her lute—
Is wondering why her lover's skiff
So slowly glides to the lonely cliff.

Row on, row on!—When the Whole is fled,
The song will be hushed, and the rapture dead;
And I must go in my grief again
To the toils of day, and the haunts of men,
To a future of fear, and a present of care,
And memory's dream of the things that were.

XIII.

One day my First young Cupid made
  In Vulcan's Lemnian cell,
For alas! he has learned his father's trade,
  As many have found too well;
He worked not the work with golden twine,
  He wreathed it not with flowers,
He left the metal to rust in the mine,
  The roses to fade in the bowers:
He forged my First of looks and sighs,
  Of painful doubts and fears,
Of passionate hopes and memories,
  Of eloquent smiles and tears.

My Second was born a wayward thing,
  Like others of his name,
With a fancy as light as the gossamer's wing,
  And a spirit as hot as flame,
And apt to trifle time away,
  And rather fool than knave,
And either very gravely gay,
  Or very gayly grave;
And far too weak, and far too wild,
  And far too free of thought,
To rend what Venus' laughing child
  On Vulcan's anvil wrought.

And alas! as he led, that festive night,
  His mistress down the stair,
And felt, by the flambeau's flickering light,
  That she was very fair,
He did not guess—as they paused to hear
  How music's dying tone
Came mournfully to the distant ear,
  With a magic all its own—
That the archer god, to thrall his soul,
  Was lingering in the porch,
Disguised that evening, like my Whole,
  With a sooty face and torch.

XIV.

When Ralph by holy hands was tied
  For life to blooming Cis,
Sir Thrifty too drove home his bride,
  A fashionable Miss,
That day, my First, with jovial sound,
  Proclaimed the happy tale,
And drunk was all the country round
  With pleasure—or with ale.

Oh, why should Hymen ever blight
  The roses Cupid wore?—
Or why should it be ever night
  Where it was day before?—
Or why should women have a tongue,
  Or why should it be cursed,
In being, like my Second, long,
  And louder than my First?

"You blackguard!" cries the rural wench,
  My lady screams, "Ah, bête!"
And Lady Thrifty scolds in French,
  And Cis in Billingsgate;
Till both their Lords my Second try,
  To end connubial strife—
Sir Thrifty hath the means to die,
  And Ralph—to beat his wife!

XV.

Lord Roland by the gay torchlight
  Held revel in his hall;
He broached my First, that jovial knight,
  And pledged his vassals tall;
The red stream went from wood to can,
  And then from can to mouth,

And the deuce a man knew how it ran,
  Nor heeded, north or south:
"Let the health go wide," Lord Ronald cried,
  As he saw the river flow—
"One cup to-night to the noblest Bride,
  And one to the stoutest foe!"

Lord Ronald kneeled, when the morning came,
  Low in his mistress' bower;
And she gave him my Second, that beauteous dame,
  For a spell in danger's hour:
Her silver shears were not at hand;
  And she smiled a playful smile,
As she cleft it with her lover's brand,
  And grew not pale the while:
And "Ride, and ride," Lord Ronald cried,
  As he kissed its auburn glow;
"For he that woos the noblest Bride
  Must beard the stoutest Foe!"

Lord Ronald stood, when the day shone fair,
  In his garb of glittering mail;
And marked how my Whole was crumbling there
  With the battle's iron hail:
The bastion and the battlement
  On many a craven crown,
Like rocks from some huge mountain rent,

Were trembling darkly down:
"Whate'er betide," Lord Ronald cried,
As he bade his trumpets blow—
"I shall win to-day the noblest Bride,
Or fall by the stoutest Foe!"

XVI.

I graced Don Pedro's revelry,
All dressed in fire and feather,
When loveliness and chivalry
Were met to feast together.
He flung the slave who moved the lid,
A purse of maravedis;
And this that gallant Spaniard did,
For me and for the ladies.

He vowed a vow, that noble knight,
Before he went to table,
To make his only sport the fight,
His only couch the stable,
Till he had dragged, as he was bid,
Five score of Turks to Cadiz;—
And this that gallant Spaniard did,
For me and for the ladies.

To ride through mountains, where my First
  A banquet would be reckoned;
Through deserts, where to quench their thirst
  Men vainly turn my Second.
To leave the gates of fair Madrid,
  To dare the gates of Hades;—
And this that gallant Spaniard did,
  For me and for the ladies.

XVII.

He talked of daggers and of darts,
  Of passions and of pains,
Of weeping eyes and wounded hearts,
  Of kisses and of chains;
He said, though love was kin to grief,
  She was not born to grieve;
He said, though many rued belief,
  She safely might believe;
But still the lady shook her head,
  And swore, by yea and nay,
My Whole was all that he had said,
  And all that he could say.

He said, my First—whose silent car
  Was slowly wandering by,
Veiled in a vapour faint and far
  Through the unfathomed sky—
Was like the smile whose rosy light
  Across her young lips passed,
Yet oh! it was not half so bright,
  It changed not half so fast;
But still the lady shook her head,
  And swore, by yea and nay,
My Whole was all that he had said,
  And all that he could say.

And then he set a cypress wreath
  Upon his raven hair,
And drew his rapier from its sheath,
  Which made the lady stare;
And said, his life-blood's purple flow
  My Second there should dim,
If she he served and worshipped so
  Would only weep for him;
But still the lady shook her head,
  And swore, by yea and nay,
My Whole was all that he had said,
  And all that he could say.

XVIII.

UNCOUTH was I of face and form,
  But strong to blast and blight,
By pestilence and thunder-storm,
  By famine and by fight;
I pierced the rivets of the mail,
  I maimed the war-steed's hoof,
I bade the yellow harvest fail,
And sent the blast to rend the sail,
  And the bolt to rend the roof.

Within my Second's dark recess
  In silent pomp I dwelt,
Before the mouth in lowliness
  My rude adorers knelt;
'Twas a fearful place; a pile of stones
  Stood for its stately door;
Its music was of sighs and groans,
And the torch-light fell on human bones
  Unburied on the floor!

The chieftain, ere his band he led,
  Came thither with his prayer;
The boatman, ere his sail he spread,
  Watched for an omen there;

And ever the shriek rang loud within,
  And ever the red blood ran,
And amid the sin and smoke and din
I sate with a changeless, endless grin,
  Forging my First for Man!

My priests are rotting in their grave,
  My shrine is silent now;
There is no victim in my cave,
  No crown upon my brow;
Nothing is left but dust and clay
  Of all that was divine;
My name and my memory pass away,
But dawn and dusk of one fair day
  Are called by mortals mine.

XIX.

My First to-night in young Haidee
  Is so surpassing fair,
That, though my Second precious be,
  It shows all faded there;
And let my Whole be never twined
  To shame those beaming charms,
A richer one she cannot find
  Than fond Affection's arms.

(1826.)

XX.

He who can make my First to roll
  When not a breath is blowing,
May very slightly turn my Whole
  To set a mountain going.

He who can curb my Second's will
  When she's inclined for roving,
May turn my Whole more slightly still
  To cure the moon of moving!

XXI.

Across my First, with flash and roar,
  The stately vessel glides alone;
And silent on the crowded shore
  There kneels an aged crone,
Watching my Second's parting smile
As he looks farewell to his native isle.

My Whole comes back to other eyes
  With beauteous change of fruits and flowers;
But black to her are those bright skies,
  And sad those joyous bowers;
Alas! my First is dark and deep,
And my Second cannot hear her weep!

XXII.

Sir Eustace goes to the far Crusade
  In radiant armour dressed;
And my First is graven on his blade,
  And broidered on his breast.

And a flush is on his cheek and brow,
  And a fever in his blood,
As he stands upon my Second now,
  And gazes on the flood.

Away, away!—the canvas drives
  Like a sea-bird's rustling wing;
My Whole hath a score of Moslem lives
  Upon its twanging string.

XXIII.

My First came forth in booted state,
For far Valencia bound;
And smiled to feel my Second's weight,
And hear its creaking sound.

"And here's a jailer sweet," quoth he,
"You cannot bribe or cozen;
To keep one ward in custody,
Wise men will forge a dozen."

But daybreak saw a lady ride
My Whole across the plain,
With a handsome cavalier beside,
To hold her bridle-rein:

And "Blessing on the bonds," quoth he,
"Which wrinkled age imposes,
If woman must your prisoner be,
Your chain should be of roses."

XXIV.

Oh yes! her childhood hath been nursed
In all the follies of my First;
And why doth she turn from the glittering throng,
From the Courtier's jest, and the Minstrel's song?

Why doth she look where the ripples play
Around my Second in yon fair bay,
While the boat in the twilight nears the shore,
With her speechless crew, and her muffled oar?

Hath she not heard in her lonely bower
My Whole's fond tale of magic power?
Softer and sweeter that music flows
Than the Bulbul's hymn to the midnight rose.

XXV.

My First, that was so fresh and fair,
  Hath faded—faded from thy face;
  And pale Decay hath left no trace
Of bloom and beauty there.

And round that virgin heart of thine
  My Second winds his cold caress;
  That virgin heart, whose tenderness
Was Passion's purest shrine,

Roses are springing on thy clay;
  And there my Whole, obscurely bright,
  Still shows his little lamp by night,
And hides it still by day.

Aptly it decks that cypress bower,
  For even thus thy faith was proved,
  Most clearly seen, most fondly loved,
In Sorrow's darkest hour.

XXVI.

When my First flings down o'er tower and town
  Its sad and solemn veil,
When the tempests sweep o'er the angry deep,
  And the stars are ghastly pale,
And the gaunt wolves howl to the answering
    owl
  In the pause of the fitful gale,

My Second will come to his ancient home
  From his dark and narrow bed;
His warrior heel is cased in steel,
  But ye cannot bear its tread;
And the beaming brand is in his hand,
  But ye need not fear the dead.

Through battle and blast his bark had passed,
  O'er many a stormy tide;
He had burst in twain the tyrant's chain,
  He had won the beauteous bride;
From the field of fame unscathed he came,
  And by my Whole he died.

(1827.)

XXVII.

Up, up, Lord Raymond, to the fight!
  Gird on thy bow of yew!
And see thy javelin's point be bright,
  Thy falchion's temper true;
For over the hill and over the vale
My First is pouring its iron hail.

No craven he! yet beaten back
  From the field of death he fled;
My Second yawned upon his track,
  The lion's lonely bed;
He smote the Monarch in his lair,
And buried his rage and anguish there.

At dawn and dusk my Whole goes forth
  On the ladder's topmost round;
He looks to the south, he looks to the north,
  He bids the bugle sound;
But many a cheerless moon must wane,
Ere his exiled lord return again.

XXVIII.

MORNING is beaming o'er brake and bower,
Hark! to the chimes from yonder tower,
Call ye my First from her chamber now,
With her snowy veil and her jewelled brow.

Lo! where my Second, in gallant array,
Leads from his stable her beautiful bay,
Looking for her, as he curvets by,
With an arching neck and a glancing eye.

Spread is the banquet, and studied the song;
Ranged in meet order the menial throng,
Jerome is ready with book and stole,
And the maidens fling flowers, but where is
my Whole?

Look to the hill, is he climbing its side?
Look to the stream—is he crossing its tide?
Out on him, false one! he comes not yet—
Lady, forget him, yea, scorn and forget.

XXIX.

My First was dark o'er earth and air,
  As dark as she could be;
The stars that gemmed her ebon hair
  Were only two or three;
King Cole saw twice as many there
  As you or I could see.

"Away, King Cole!" mine hostess said
  "Flagon and flask are dry;
Your nag is neighing in the shed,
  For he knows a storm is nigh:"
She set my Second on his head,
  And she set it all awry.

He stood upright upon his legs;
  Long life to good King Cole!
With wine and cinnamon, ale and eggs,
  He filled a silver bowl;
He drained the draught to the very dregs,
  And he called that draught—my Whole.

XXX.

COME from my First, ay, come
  The battle dawn is nigh;
And the screaming trump and the thundering
    drum
  Are calling thee to die!
Fight as thy father fought,
  Fall as thy father fell,
Thy task is taught, thy shroud is wrought;
  So—forward! and farewell!

Toll ye, my Second! toll!
  Fling high the flambeau's light;
And sing the hymn for a parted soul,
  Beneath the silent night!
The helm upon his head,
  The cross upon his breast,
Let the prayer be said, and the tear be shed:
  Now take him to his rest!

Call ye my Whole, go, call!
  The lord of lute and lay;
And let him greet the sable pall
  With a noble song to-day;
Go, call him by his name;
  No fitter hand may crave
To light the flame of a soldier's fame
  On the turf of a soldier's grave.

(1829.)

XXXI.

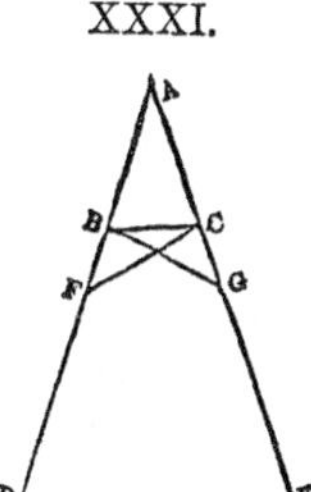

My First, in its usual quiet way,
Was creeping along on a wintry day,
When a minstrel came to its muddy bed,
With a harp on his shoulder, a wreath on his
 head;
And "How shall I cross," the poor bard cried,
"To the cloisters and courts on the other side?'

Old Euclid came; he frowned a frown;
He flung the harp and the green wreath down;
And he led the boy with a stately march
To my Second's neat and narrow Arch;
And "See," quoth the sage, "how every ass
Over the sacred stream must pass."

The youth was mournful, the youth was mute;
He sighed for his laurel, and sobbed for his lute;
The youth took courage, the youth took snuff;
He followed in faith his teacher gruff;
And he sits ever since on my Whole's kind lap,
In a silken gown, and a trencher cap.

XXXII.

An aged man, with locks of snow,
  Sits o'er his glass serenely gay;
Plain Tom, the weaver, long ago,
  Sir Thomas Clover, Knight, to-day:
My First beside his grandsire stands,
  A comely stripling, stout and tall,
The future lord of his broad lands,
  And of his hospitable hall.

"What can it mean, my pretty toy,
  With all its wheels, and threads, and springs?"
And, as he speaks, the wondering boy
  His arms around his grandsire flings:
He's puzzled, puzzled, more and more;
  And putting on a look of thought,
He turns my Second o'er and o'er,
  A silver model deftly wrought.

The good Knight hears with placid smile,
  And bids him in the plaything view
A proud memorial of the toil
  By which his grandsire's fortunes grew:
And tells them this, my Whole, shall be
  Still handed down from son to son,
To teach them by what industry
  Their titles and their lands were won.

XXXIII.

The Palmer comes from the Holy Land;
Scarce on my First can the Palmer stand:
The Prior will take the air to-day;
On my Second the Prior trots away:
'Tis pleasanter, under a summer sun,
With robes to ride, than with rags to run.

My Whole leaped out of the road-side ditch,
With "Stand!" to the poor man, and "Stand!"
to the rich:
From the Prior he strips his mantle fair;
From the Palmer he wins but pity and prayer:
'Tis safer, when crime is prowling wide,
With rags to run, than with robes to ride.

XXXIV.

O'DONOGHUE came to the hermit's cell;
He climbed the ladder, he pulled the bell;
"I have ridden," said he, "with the Saint to dine
On his richest meat, and his reddest wine."

The Hermit hasted my First to fill
With water from the limpid rill;
And "Drink," quoth he, "of the juice, brave Knight,
Which breeds no fever, and prompts no fight."

The Hermit hasted my Second to spread
With stalks of lettuce and crusts of bread;
And "Taste," quoth he, "of the cates, fair guest,
Which bring no surfeit, and break no rest."

Hasty and hungry, the Chief explored
My Whole with the point of his ready sword,
And found, as yielded the latch and lock,
A pasty of Game and a flagon of hock.

XXXV.

THE night was dark, the night was damp:
St. Bruno read by his lonely lamp.
The Fiend dropped in to make a call,
As he posted away to a fancy ball;
And "Can't I find," said the Father of lies,
"Some present a Saint may not despise?"

Wine he brought him, such as yet
Was ne'er on Pontiff's table set:
Weary and faint was the holy man,
But he crossed with a cross the Tempter's can,
And saw, ere my First to his parched lip came,
That it was red with liquid flame.

Jewels he showed him—many a gem
Fit for a Sultan's diadem:
Dazzled, I trow, was the anchorite:
But he told his beads with all his might;
And instead of my Second, so rich and rare,
A pinch of worthless dust lay there.

A Lady at last he handed in,
With a bright black eye and a fair white skin:
The stern ascetic flung, 'tis said,
A ponderous missal at her head:
She vanished away; and what a smell
Of my Whole she left in the hermit's cell!

XXXVI.

Upon my First's blue stream
  The moon's cold light is sleeping;
And Marion in her mournful dream
  Is wandering there and weeping.
Where is my Whole?—this hour
  His boat should cleave the water;
He is a Knight of pride and power,
  But he loves the Huntsman's daughter.

The shroud her marriage vest—
  The stone her nuptial pillow—
So, in my Second let her rest,
  Beneath the grieving willow.
Where is my Whole?—go, Song,
  Go, solemn Song, to chide him;
His hall lets in a revelling throng,
  And a gay bride smiles beside him!

(August, 1829.)

XXXVII.

He hath seen the tempest lower:
  He hath dared the foeman's spear;
He hath welcomed Death on tide and tower;
  How will he greet him here?
My First was set, and in his place
  You might see the dark man stand,
With a fearful vizor on his face,
  And a bright axe in his hand.

Short shrift, and hurried prayer:
  Now bid the pale priest go;
And let my Second be bound and bare
  To meet the fatal blow.
The dark man grinned in bitter scorn;
  And you might hear him say,
"It was black as jet but yestermorn,
  Whence is it white to-day?"

"Rise! thou art pardoned!"—vain!
  Lift up the lifeless clay;
On the skin no scratch, on the steel no stain,—
  But the soul hath passed away.
The dark man laid his bright axe by
  As he heard the tower clock chime;
And he thought that none but my Whole would
    die
  A minute before the time.

(July, 1829.)

XXXVIII.

THERE hangs a picture in an ancient hall:
  A group of hunters meeting in their joy
On a green lawn; the gladdest of them all
  Is old Sir Geoffrey's heir, a bright-eyed boy.
A little girl has heard the bugle call,
  And she is running from her task or toy
To whisper caution: on the pony bounds,
And see, my First steals off before the hounds.

There is another picture;—that wild youth
  Is grown to manhood; by the great salt lake
He clasps his new sword on; and gentle Ruth
  Smiles, smiles and sobs as if her heart would break,
And talks right well of constancy and truth,
  And bids him keep my Second for her sake,—
A precious pledge that, wander where he will,
One heart will think and dream about him still.

And yet another picture; from far lands
  The truant is returned; but ah, his bride,
Sickness hath marred her beauty! mute he stands,
  Mute in the darkened chamber by her side;

And brings the medicine, sweetest from those hands,
  Still whispering hope which she would check or chide.
Doth the charmed cup recall the fainting soul
E'en from Death's grasp! oh! blessings on my Whole!

(1881.)

THE END.